Alfred Presents . . .

PRACTICE & PERFORMANCE

A Practice Guide for Students
to Accompany *Masterwork Classics*

Level 3

BY

JANE MAGRATH

May be used with Lesson Book 3 of *Alfred's Basic Piano Library*.

Start *Masterwork Classics 3* after page 22 in Lesson Book 3.

CONTENTS

Written for the student, **Practice and Performance 3** gives practice guides for each piece in *Masterwork Classics 3*. Brief notes for the teacher also appear for each selection.

The student should use this volume as his practice guide at home or in the practice room. When individual lesson time is short, it can help the teacher by organizing effective student practice techniques. The teacher should check the student's answers to the questions posed for each piece. Also, points made in the section "Notes to the Teacher" can save lesson time by giving the teacher a focus in presenting the piece.

Instructors of piano pedagogy courses in colleges and universities might elect to use this volume as a class text or workbook. It makes available for the prospective piano teacher, as does no other book currently available, structured information that a piano student should receive when playing particular pieces from the standard repertoire. In essence it is a "method" for playing the classics.

The language used in this commentary volume is not "watered-down" for the young piano student. It is important that the young students, as well as older pre-college and adult students, learn to speak intelligently and with correct terminology about music. Students who tested this volume began to display a consistent thought process in practice procedures and, perhaps even more importantly, an increased awareness of the importance of listening to themselves in practice — of hearing what they play.

Practical Uses for the Practice Guide

Teachers will have specific and differing purposes for using this commentary volume with each student. Recognizing the personal needs of many students, as well as various teaching styles and personal preferences, several possible modes for the use of *Practice and Performance* are listed below.

1. For Student Study both at home and at the lesson. This is an ideal situation for using this volume. The written questions and the commentary for each piece can be reinforced by the teacher, who will emphasize important concepts and will stress other points from the volume as he/she prefers . This usage can serve as a springboard for more detailed historical as well as theoretical study.

2. For Student Study independent from the lesson. Some teachers will prefer to have students work from this volume at home during practice. The volume is written to be self-explanatory for students. It is a practice and listening guide for students.

3. For "Preparation" of Student Literature before assigning it. Teachers may want to use the volume only for the section titled "Preparing for Performance" to mentally and visually prepare students for each piece before beginning study on it. This insures that the student does not begin a score without a guide as to the mood, meaning, and structure of the music.

4. For Reinforcement of Aural Goals. Teachers may use the final section separately for each piece. "Finishing the Performance" provides questions a student can ask himself/herself about the performance of the piece. It is designed to help him know what to listen for in the final stages of perfecting a piece. The goal of this section is to develop the skill of listening to oneself and the knowledge of what to listen for. The student should practice using this series of questions "with his/her ear as the teacher."

Practice and performance suggestions for each selection in *Masterwork Classics 3* are given in this order:

GETTING READY TO PLAY — preparation

PRACTICING FOR PERFORMANCE — playing

FINISHING FOR PERFORMANCE — evaluating what was heard and reworking the performance

• **Getting ready to play** suggests elements that a student should consider before he/she begins to play a piece. This section helps the student prepare before beginning to practice. The student learns <u>how</u> to look at a new score and <u>what</u> to look for in it. For each piece, the student first establishes what the character, mood, affect (for Baroque literature), or feeling of the piece should be. He/she writes answers to specific questions in the practice guide.

The student also scans the score to observe considerations such as the basic form, appearances of repetitions, strong cadential areas, phrase structure, and unusual fingerings. From the beginning the student is asked to determine a musical plan — a shape for each phrase. This is accomplished by asking him/her to write brackets around the phrases in the music in *Masterwork Classics* such as this ⌈   ⌉. Open brackets are placed at beginnings and endings of phrases in the margin above the treble clef. The student then is asked to place an arrow ↓ above the note or harmony of greatest tension in the phrase. This is explained in one of several ways. This point of tension may be defined as the "magnet note" (the note to which all notes preceding it pull), the "focal point," the "peak" of the phrase, the "goal" of a phrase, the "point of greatest tension," or the "strongest chord."

• **Practicing for performance** presents a viable practice plan to use in working on a particular piece. It suggests to a student what to do, how to do it, and in what order. It gives him/her guidelines along the way to help his/her ear know when to move on to the next step. Of course, teachers may alter the order of steps presented or alter the practice plan. This detailed plan allows the student to know exactly what to do in working out each piece. Consistent with the philosophy of the entire volume, directions often are given in a manner that directs the student to move ahead when he/she "hears" a certain point accomplished.

• **Finishing for performance** is totally aurally oriented in focus. Its goal is to teach students how to listen to themselves by suggesting points for which to listen. Most of the questions begin "Do you hear...?" The pianist lets his/her ear be the guide ("the teacher") in working toward specific aural goals.

The questions that ask what the student "hears" in performance are an attempt to direct the listening. Since our goal is always to be able to "hear what we play," it follows that students need to know <u>what</u> it is that they listen for in the music. This goal reflects the focus of the questions in this section.

Music in the literature volumes is carefully sequenced and structured so that
1. concepts are presented gradually through standard literature
2. concepts build upon each other and are reinforced
3. the number of concepts found in a piece increases in a gradually paced way rather than haphazardly

For these reasons, it is suggested that repertoire in each period be taught in the order of the list at the front of the volume. A student will work with pieces from at least two of the periods at the same time as reflected in the parallel columns.

Sequential Presentation

SUGGESTED ORDER OF STUDY

The repertoire may be taught in this sequence to allow playing requirements for each piece to build upon skills developed in earlier repertoire in *Masterwork Classics 3.*

Literature is listed in two columns since most students will study at least two pieces from this book simultaneously. This dual list allows contrast of style and sound for the student.

affect — the feeling or mood that the music or a part of the music portrays

Alberti bass — accompaniment figure based on broken chords and used in many sonatinas and sonatas; named after Domenico Alberti

allegretto — moderately fast; tempo between andante and allegro

allegro — happy

AMB Notebook (Anna Magdalena Bach Notebook) — Anna Magdalena, the wife of J. S. Bach, received this notebook from her husband for her twenty-fourth birthday. In it she wrote many of the favorite pieces of the members of the Bach family circle. Several of these pieces which are included in *Masterwork Classics* have become quite popular Baroque pieces.

andante — walking tempo

Anh. (Anhang) — found sometimes in the numbering of a piece by a composer, it refers to the appendix of the thematic listing of the works of that composer

animato — animated

articulation markings — signs for legato, staccato, and other indications for the lengths and groupings of notes

balance — used here to refer to relative loudness of the melody to the accompaniment

binary form — form of a piece having two sections, each of which is repeated

BWV Anh. (Bach Werke Verzeichnis Anhang — Catalog of Bach's Works — Supplement) —the listing of Bach's complete works in the Schmieder thematic catalog

brackets (⌈   ⌉) — signs to be used in the margin above the treble clef to enclose phrases

cadence — chords (or melody) at the conclusion of a phrase, a section, or a piece that give the impression of an ending

con moto — with motion

Dal Segno al Fine (D. S. al Fine) — designation to go back to the sign and play to the end

deciso — decisive

dolce — sweetly

écossaise — dance in quick 2/4 time popular in the 19th century

energico — with energy

focal point — used here to refer to the note(s) or harmony that sounds like the point of greatest tension and importance in a phrase; it is often the peak or loudest point in a phrase

fermata (⌢) — pause; hold the tone or silence beyond the indicated time value

Fine — end

form — the plan for a piece, similar in some ways to an architect's plan for a house

giocoso — humorous

Hob. (Hoboken) — refers to Hoboken's thematic catalog of all of Haydn's works; the numbering of Haydn's music is based on this catalog

imitation — repetition of a phrase or fragment

K. (Kochel) — refers to Kochel's Thematic List of the Complete Works of Mozart; the numbering of Mozart's music is based on this catalog and later additions and revisions

legato — smooth and connected

ma non troppo — but not too much

maestoso — majestically

marcato — marked, accented

marziale — martial

menuet — graceful dance in moderate triple meter

moderato — in a moderate tempo

mordent (⋀⋁) — musical ornament consisting of three notes, the written note, the note immediately below it, and the repetition of the written note

motive — short figure (rhythmic or melodic) that recurs throughout a composition. It is usually much shorter than a theme.

nicht schnell — not fast

ornament — sign for a quick inflection of notes such as the trill and the mordent

perpendosi — dying away

phrase — a division of music, similar to a sentence

più —more

poco — little

portato — manner of performance halfway between staccato and legato

programmatic — music which is influenced by an idea that is non—musical. It may be indicated in title or described in a preface. The program for a piece might be a mood set by the composer's title or it might be a story told through the music.

scherzando — playful

senza — without

symmetry — balance of parts

tapering the end of a phrase — lessening of sound at the end of a phrase

tempo di marcia — tempo of a march

vivace — lively

vivo — lively

voicing — bringing out a note or a melody above other notes in the musical texture

tranquillo — tranquil

trill — ornament consisting of the alternation of a note with the note above it

WoO (Works without opus number) — Numbering of Beethoven's works for which he did not leave an opus number

Baroque Period

What is "Priming for the Pinnacle?"

We all want to get to the "pinnacle!" The pinnacle is the highest point. The pinnacle of a mountain looks inviting from down below. And then when we reach it — by car, by hiking, by a tram or ski lift — it is even more breathtaking and exciting than we had ever imagined!

Someone who is "priming" for a goal is "getting ready, preparing" for that goal. In a sense, we are "priming for the pinnacle" in everything we do! That is exactly what this book helps you do. It is written to help the performer work toward stylistic and top quality performances — with every piece he/she plays.

Each piece has a guide to help the student learn to think, listen, and concentrate. It is a practice guide, a rudimentary analysis guide, and a listening guide. It is a step in helping students learn what they can do in practice.

Doctrine of Affections — What is the "Affect?"

The first thing to think about with any Baroque piece in this section is "what is the mood or affect of this piece?" In Baroque music most pieces have a certain feeling or affection that continues through the entire piece. To decide from the onset what affect we feel the composer meant the piece to convey makes all of the practice on that piece aim toward that feeling or mood. It creates an emotional and "sound" goal for the performer to strive to convey from the beginning.

Rhythm in the Baroque

Many pieces written in the Baroque were based on different kinds of dances. These dances had specific characteristics that make them individual, just as you might imagine that the waltz and the menuet are very different. One of the best ways to make a dance come alive is to play with buoyant and steady rhythm.

Strong rhythm actually is at the heart of all Baroque music and style. The rhythm is often continuous and lively. It needs strong definition and energy. The movement is forward-looking, and often it seems that Baroque music rattles off one phrase after another with a lively underpinning rhythmic figure. In performance of all Baroque music, be aware of this underpinning so that it keeps your performance vital and hearty.

Dynamics and the Baroque Harpsichord

While crescendo and diminuendo were impossible on the harpsichord, Baroque composers undoubtedly intended phrase shaping and nuance in the music they wrote. Some instruments such as the violin and the human voice (the singer) could give this nuance easily. It seems that we limit the piano as an instrument unnecessarily if we perform Baroque music without an arch or nuance to the phrase. The answer is to not over-do the phrasing. A teacher can be most helpful in molding a piece into a tasteful, stylistic performance.

Since the harpsichord was able to add and subtract blocks of sound through "couplings" and changes of manual, the sound of the harpsichord could be loud, then suddenly soft, and so on. We can imitate this in our performances today by including sudden changes of dynamics where the harpsichordist might have changed manuals or where he/she might have echoed a repeated phrase on a different manual.

Listed for each piece are performance considerations which are emphasized in each selection

Baroque Literature

Petit Rondo .... Geoffroy
- detailed articulation
- independence between hands

Petit Menuet .... Geoffroy
- detailed articulation
- independence between hands

Air, BWV Anh. 114 .... AMB Notebook
- detailed articulation
- preparation for contrapuntal playing
- left hand expansion
- fingering principles

Menuet en Rondeau .... Rameau
- balance of melody and rapidly moving accompaniment
- left hand expansion and contraction
- technical facility
- movement about the keyboard
- feeling for octaves

Passepied in C Major .... Handel
- expansion and contraction
- detailed articulation
- preparation for contrapuntal style

Menuet in G Major, BWV Anh. 114 .... AMB Notebook
- preparation for contrapuntal style
- fingering shifts
- control of legato and nuance in a phrase

Petit Rondo

Geoffroy

See *Masterwork Classics 3*, page 4.

Getting ready to play

*(Write the answers in this book and on the music in **Masterwork Classics**.)*

Composers of Baroque period music often had a mood or affect in mind for each piece. Usually the affect continued through an entire piece. There were no strong changes of mood within that selection. Sight-read the right hand melody and decide on an affect that you think fits "Petit Rondo." The affect will be a descriptive word like "cheerful," "happy," or "stately." Write it in the blank you find here. _____ When you practice, one of your main goals will be to play the music so that the way you play the piece describes that affect or mood to someone who does not know what affect you have chosen.

Sight-read the melody in the right hand. Listen to find out which notes should be included in each phrase or musical sentence. Place an open bracket (⌈   ⌉) at the beginning and end of each phrase in your music book, *Masterwork Classics 3*. Write in the margin above the treble clef.

Play and sing the melody again several times. Try to determine which is the most important note in each phrase. The music will seem to pull to this note. Sometimes it is the highest note, but this is not always the case. That note (or chord) will be called the focal point, the magnet note, or the peak of the phrase. Writing again in your music book, place a small arrow above the focal point in each phrase. When you practice, you will strive to play so that the phrase pulls to this note. Usually a slight crescendo to this point and slight diminuendo afterward helps to show the focal point.

The "D. C. al Fine" at the end indicates that the performer should go back to the beginning and play to the end. If you label the first line <u>a</u> and the second line <u>b</u>, then the form (or composer's plan) for this piece is <u>a</u> <u>b</u> <u>a</u>.

Writing in the blanks below, mark the dynamic level for each section of this piece.

a _____
b _____
a _____

Practicing for performance

(Answer the questions in your mind and through the way you practice.)

Practice step by step. Be sure that you do not move ahead until you have met all of the thought and sound goals for the previous step that you worked on. These goals come from what you have learned about earlier pieces as well as what you find written in the step. Your ear will tell you when you have learned a step well enough to move ahead! At the beginning of your practice the following day, you will want to go back several steps to practice and review what you have learned in earlier practice.

1. Practice the right hand alone in measures 1-4. Select a tempo that is sufficiently slow to allow you to hear the correct articulation (staccatos and slurs) and to check on your fingering. Practice making the phrase pull to the focal point. Then practice the left hand alone working for the same goals.

2. Combine both hands in measures 1-4. Listen carefully for the same goals as above. Check to be certain that all fingerings are correct. If you are inaccurate when playing the fingering or other details, take a slower tempo so that your hands can keep up with your mind.

3. Learn the second line, measures 5-8, by practicing the same way that you did in steps 1 and 2 above.

4. Combine the sections of this piece. Play slowly at first. Practice to hear the different dynamic levels for each line. When you can play "Petit Rondo" correctly at the slow tempo, increase it gradually until you can perform up to tempo. Practice to make your performance describe the affect you have chosen.

Finishing for performance

(Answer the questions in your mind.) Ask yourself:

Do you hear your performance describe the affect you decided upon?

Do you hear the focal point in each phrase?

Do you hear light staccatos and all of the articulation markings in the score?

Do you hear the dynamic differences for each line?

Do you hear one or two pulses per measure rather than four pulses?

Now practice so that you are able to answer "yes" to each of these questions. Let your ear listen when you practice and tell you whether you could answer "yes" to each question. Change your way of playing when you need to so that the answer becomes "yes."

To the Teacher

Affect: dancing
Fingering: left hand spans an octave
Phrase definition: regular
Coordination: articulation of two-note slurs against left hand held notes

This piece helps a student learn:
• independence between the hands

Notes:
The first step in student practice should be to determine an affect for each piece. Doing this places the student's emphasis in practice on expressing a mood or feeling through the music. The student should look for the meaning that the music could have to him/her and to those who listen. Then in practicing, he/she should aim to achieve that affect or mood.

Questions to the student asking him/her to hear one pulse for each measure are designed to help avoid performances which lack flow of the phrase and forward movement. The avoidance of frequent accents is important.

Petit Menuet

Geoffroy

See *Masterwork Classics 3*, page 4.

Getting ready to play

Sight-read the right hand melody. Decide what affect or mood you feel the composer wanted to convey. Write that affect in this book in the space provided. _____

Place brackets around the phrases or musical sentences in this piece. Sometimes either of two answers could be correct. The phrases in this piece are each three measures long. Do you hear the phrase sound like a sentence in music when you play the melody? _____ It is important to group the notes in a phrase together when you practice.

What notes are different between the first phrase and the second phrase? _____ What notes are different between the third phrase and the fourth phrase? _____ (Notice the small difference in the left hand between measure 8 and measure 11.) How many different measures do you have to learn to play this piece? _____

Write here the dynamic marking for each phrase in "Petit Menuet."

phrase one   _____
phrase two   _____
phrase three _____
phrase four _____

Sight-read the right hand melody again and sing as you play. Decide where the focal point occurs for each phrase and place an arrow in your music book above that note.

Practicing for performance

Practice step by step. Be sure that you do not move ahead until you have met all of the thought and sound goals for the previous step that you worked on. These goals come from what you have learned about earlier pieces as well as what you find written in the step. Your ear will tell you when you have learned a step well enough to move ahead! At the beginning of your practice the following day, you will want to go back several steps to practice and review what you have learned in earlier practice.

1. Practice the first phrase hands separately. Listen for and think about
   - correct fingering
   - articulation
   - focal point of the phrase

Continue by practicing hands together and aiming for all of these same goals.

2. Combine both phrases in line one. Listen especially for the dynamic contrast between the phrases as well as for the goals listed in No. 1.

3. Practice line two in the same way that you practiced in Nos. 1 and 2 above. Be certain to continue to listen for sound goals and to work to hear dynamic differences.

4. Combine both sections of the piece. Remember to play first at a tempo that is sufficiently slow so that you play everything correctly. Then gradually increase the tempo. Listen to make your playing convey the affect that you decided upon.

Finishing for performance

Ask yourself:

Do you hear one pulse per measure?
Do you hear the dynamic differences between phrases?
Do you hear the focal point of the phrase?
Do you hear light staccatos?

Practice now so that your answer to all of these questions is "yes." Your ear and mind will help you with the practice.

To the Teacher

Affect: cheerful; like walking on tiptoe

Fingering: each hand is independent of the other

Phrase definition: three-measure phrases are an unusual feature

Coordination: this piece prepares for contrapuntal playing

This piece helps a student develop:
- independence between the hands
- articulation of short ideas

Notes:
Correct fingering of this piece is important since the hands play independently of one another.

Air, BWV Anh. 131

from AMB Notebook

See *Masterwork Classics 3*, page 5.

Getting ready to play

After sight-reading the melody of this piece and observing the tempo indication, write the mood or affect that you think it should have. _____

Label the two sections of this piece A and B. Does the melody in the B section seem to be similar to the melody in the A section? Or does the melody in the B section seem to be a different theme from the A section? _____

Compare the rhythm of lines two and four. Even though the notes are not the same, the similarity of the rhythm holds this piece together. Listen for this as you learn it.

You should notice that all quarter notes, except those with a slur over them, are played portato. Portato notes are usually played one-half of the length of the note—so here the portatos would sound more or less like "long" eighth notes. Also, the staccatos in measures 12 and 13 indicate that the half notes should be played as quarters with a rest after them.

The ends of cadences in this piece all have wide bass leaps which outline the chord and make the feeling of the key even stronger. Circle the bass skips in measures 3, 6, 7, 11, 14, and 15.

Place brackets around the phrases in this piece. You will notice that all four phrases begin with an upbeat (on beat 4). Be sure you group the upbeat with the correct phrase. Notice that the first phrase is unusual in that it is three measures long—not four or two.

Now place arrows above the treble staff over the magnet note or focal point in each phrase. The magnet note in these phrases could be the highest melody note in each phrase. But other notes could work equally well in some phrases. Play the melody and sing the tune several times for each phrase before making your choice. In this piece, and in all of them, you may change your mind and move the arrow while practicing. Your ear is the best guide.

Practicing for performance

Practice step by step. Be sure that you do not move ahead until you have met all of the thought and sound goals for the previous step that you worked on. These goals come from what you have learned about earlier pieces as well as what you find written in the step. Your ear will tell you when you have learned a step well enough to move ahead! At the beginning of your practice the following day, you will want to go back several steps to practice and review what you have learned in earlier practice.

1. Practice each hand separately in the first phrase to
   • achieve the correct fingering
   • achieve and hear the phrase pulling to the arrow
   • achieve and hear the correct articulation

2. Practice the first phrase hands together <u>very slowly</u> but perfectly. Keep taking a slower and slower tempo if necessary until you can play it correctly several times in a row. Gradually ease the tempo into a faster one. Listen for the same three points as in No. 1.

3. Practice the other three phrases as you did in steps 1 and 2.

4. Practice the cadences in measures 6-7, measures 10-11, and measures 14-15 until they feel and sound very solid and definite.

5. Combine the phrases so that you play the A section as a whole and then the B section.

6. Work slowly at first and then gradually increase the tempo as you combine the sections, to get the entire piece up to performance level.

Finishing for performance

Ask yourself:

Do you play so that the listener will hear the phrase endings and know where the phrases are?

Do you hear the rise and fall of each phrase?

Do you hear the lightness of this piece, almost like a dance?

Do you hear the flow of the pulse rather than frequent accents?

Does your performance convey the mood or affect you decided on?

To the Teacher

Affect: noble, courtly

Fingering: to be noted are several uses of non-consecutive fingers (1 3) on consecutive keys

Number of ideas: melodic material different throughout

Phrase definition: regular except for the first three-measure idea; 3 + 4 + 4 + 4

Coordination: both hands often in disjunct movement

This piece helps a student learn:
- coordination of disjunct motion
- leaps in left hand
- fingering principles

Notes:

The teacher should be sure the student hears the three-measure phrase as a musical unit. Phrases in this piece need a strong sense of continuity through the entire phrase.

The finger shift in both hands on beat 4 of measure 11 is important to set the hand positions for the next notes in the passage.

Variation of the dynamic level of the repeats makes the performance more interesting. This principle may be applied to many Baroque pieces.

Menuet en Rondeau   Rameau

See *Masterwork Classics 3*, page 6.

Getting ready to play

What word can you use to describe the mood or affect of this piece? _____

In which measures does the right hand not play eighth notes? _____ You might guess that these measures mark major cadences. In which measures does the right hand have other note values in addition to eighth notes? _____ You might guess that these measures are ends of phrases and cadences.

Place brackets around the phrases. Sight-read the right hand melody part to help do that.

Label the sections of this piece using <u>a</u>, <u>a'</u>, <u>b</u>, and <u>b'</u>. The ' after a letter means that the section has been changed only slightly. Also, notice that <u>b</u> and <u>b'</u> are the same as <u>a</u> and <u>a'</u>—except they are transposed to another key. Note the D.C. al Fine at the end of measure 16, indicating that the <u>a</u> and <u>a'</u> are to be repeated. The phrases of this piece in order are <u>a</u> <u>a'</u> <u>b</u> <u>b'</u> <u>a</u> <u>a'</u>.

Place an arrow above the treble staff over the note that seems to be the most important one in each phrase. Does this occur in the same place in each phrase? _____ It could. It would work to have the music pull to the beginning of the third measure in each phrase. You will find that this happens often in other pieces as well.

What is the difference between the right hand parts in lines one and two? _____ What is the difference between the left hand parts in lines one and two? _____ What is the difference between the right hand parts in lines three and four? _____ What is the difference between the left hand parts in lines three and four? _____ What is the difference between lines one and three? _____ What is the difference between lines two and four? _____

What is the dynamic plan for each line in this piece?

A   line one   _____
    line two   _____
B   line three _____
    line four   _____
A   line one   _____
    line two   _____

Practicing for performance

Practice step by step. Be sure that you do not move ahead until you have met all of the thought and sound goals for the previous step that you worked on. These goals come from what you have learned about earlier pieces as well as what you find written in the step. Your ear will tell you when you have learned a step well enough to move ahead! At the beginning of your practice the following day, you will want to go back several steps to practice and review what you have learned in earlier practice.

1. While following the exact fingering, practice the right hand alone on line one, phrasing so that the music pulls to the focal note of the phrase. Practice the left hand in the same way. Then practice line two, hands separately in the same way.

2. Slowly, play both hands together on line one listening to achieve
- no stumbles
- smooth legato
- phrases that pull to the focal note

When you hear that you have accomplished these three goals, do the same thing for line two.

3. Work on lines one and two hands together slowly until you can play each several times in a row hearing no stumbles (try for five repetitions with no mistakes). Then learn the A section with no stumbles. Listen and strive for the following in your practice:
- smooth legato in the right hand
- the same fingering each time
- shaping the phrase toward the first beat of the third measure

4. Follow the same procedure as in Nos. 1-3 above for the B section.

5. When each section is perfected seperately, put the A and B sections together, remembering that you must repeat the A section. Since you know that the A section will be played more often, practice the B section extra times. Be sure to hold the tied D in measures 15-16.

Finishing for performance

Ask yourself:

Do your phrases flow so that you hear one pulse in each measure?

Do your phrases move toward the third measure? The strongest harmony and magnet note seem to occur here.

Do you hear different dynamics for each line (the way you planned in the first section above)?

Does your playing convey the affect you decided on?

If your answer to any of these questions is "no," practice, using your ear to tell you when you have worked these things in and have accomplished your goal.

To the Teacher

Affect: happy, song-like

Fingering: left hand extensions to octave; left hand contraction and expansion

Number of ideas: one melodic idea

Phrase definition: extremely regular; predictable

Phrases coordination: right hand eighth notes against left hand quarters and halves

This piece helps a student develop:
- left hand expansion and contraction
- technical facility
- kinesthetic feeling for octaves

Passepied in C Major   Handel

See *Masterwork Classics 3*, page 7.

Getting ready to play

A passepied is a happy, spirited dance. Sight-read the right hand melody. Find several adjectives that could fit the mood of the piece. Write in this book the one word that best describes the mood or affect. _____

Play each hand separately to observe the fingering. Write in any additional fingering that you need.

How many sections do you find in "Passepied?" _____ Label them A and B. Do the A and B sections look different? _____ Which one has faster note values than the other? _____

Write the measure numbers where the left hand mimics (imitates) the right hand. _____

In measures 1, 2, and 3, notes played on which beats will be staccato? _____

At the end of a phrase, you often hear a strong cadence. This is where the composer sets the key with strong, clear chords. Two important cadences occur at the ends of sections. Name the measures. _____ When you practice, listen carefully to hear the chords pull here.

The B section begins with a new motive (a very short theme). Circle it in measure 7 in *Masterwork Classics*. Then circle all additional places that you see the motive.

How long are the phrases? _____ Mark them with open brackets in your music book. Above the treble staff, place an arrow over the most important note (the magnet note or peak) of each phrase.

Practicing for performance

Practice step by step. Be sure that you do not move ahead until you have met all of the thought and sound goals for the previous step that you worked on. These goals come from what you have learned about earlier pieces as well as what you find written in the step. Your ear will tell you when you have learned a step well enough to move ahead! At the beginning of your practice the following day, you will want to go back several steps to practice and review what you have learned in earlier practice.

1. In measures 1-4, play the first two beats only of each measure. Do this until you can play them
    • with correct fingering
    • hearing two-note slurs with a stress on the first note
    • hearing consistent rhythm in 3/4 (rest on beat 3).
Do this in the mood of the piece.

2. In the B section, measures 7-14, play the motive each time it appears
    • in tempo listening for no stops
    • with the correct fingering

3. Practice the two cadences (measures 5 and 6 and measures 13 and 14) hands together until
- the fingering is correct
- you hear the correct articulation
- you hear no stumbles

4. Practice No. 1 again.

5. Work on measures 4, 11, and 12 separately to be sure that you hear the exact articulation in the score.

6. Practice measures 1-6 hands together until the phrase pulls toward the arrow you placed in the music.

7. Work out measures 7-12 (with upbeat) hands together very slowly until this part has
- every fingering correct
- correct articulation
- the affect or mood

8. Practice the entire piece slowly. Listen and correct any mistakes. Gradually work it up to tempo.

Finishing for performance

Ask yourself:

Is all fingering correct? Is it the same each time?

Do you hear all phrases pull to the arrow (magnet note)?

Do you hear strong cadences?

Do you hear very light staccatos?

Do you hear the left-hand imitation brought out in measures 8 and 10?

Do you feel the lilt of a dance in this piece?

Do you change dynamics for the repeat?

Do you convey the mood or affect of this piece?

Practice in a way that allows your answer to become "yes" for each of these questions.

To the Teacher

Affect: sprightly

Fingering: expansion and contraction from set hand positions

Phrase definition: irregular but audible by the student (6 + 2 + 2 + 4)

Coordination: generally note-against-note texture

This piece helps a student develop:
- fingering accuracy
- coordination
- phrase movement in dances

Notes:
The student might want to repeat both sections as echos to achieve contrast.

The correct fingering, established in the early stages of working on this piece, is especially important.

Menuet in G Major, BWV Anh. 114

See *Masterwork Classics 3*, page 8.

See *Masterwork Classics 3*, page 9.

Getting ready to play

What is the mood or affect of this piece? _____ You may have heard this selection played before!

Find the two major sections of this piece and label them A and B.

The last two lines of section A are almost like the first lines. Circle the two measures in both sections in which the melodies are completely different. Did you notice that the circled measures are strong cadences (ends of sections within A)? _____

Compare the left hand of lines one and two with three and four of the first page.

The A and B sections each divide into two small sections. Mark them in your music on *Masterwork Classics*.

	Large sections	Small sections
measures 1-8	A	a
measures 9-16		a'
measures 17-24	B	b
measures 25-32		c

Play through the melody in the right hand and place brackets around the phrases. Are all of your phrases four measures long? _____ When you practice you can divide your phrases into shorter phrases to practice (two measures each) just as you divided the larger sections of this piece into smaller ones.

Place arrows above the magnet notes in each phrase.

Practicing for performance

Practice step by step. Be sure that you do not move ahead until you have met all of the thought and sound goals for the previous step that you worked on. These goals come from what you have learned about earlier pieces as well as what you find written in the step. Your ear will tell you when you have learned a step well enough to move ahead! At the beginning of your practice the following day, you will want to go back several steps to practice and review what you have learned in earlier practice.

1. For the first two measure phrase only, practice the right hand to hear and accomplish
   • correct fingering
   • correct articulation
   • phrasing and pull to the magnet note
Now do the same thing with the left hand. Then play hands together, slowly until these things are perfect several times consecutively. Your ear will tell you. Then slightly increase the tempo.

2. Follow the same steps as in No. 1 for the a' section on this page.

3. Work on the entire first page. You will want to have smooth phrasing with no punched notes and a legato sound. Be certain that you hear staccatos exactly in the right places. Check fingering carefully!

4. Follow the same procedure for learning the second page as you did with the first. This page is more intricate and may take longer to learn. Be very careful to hear and accomplish
- accurate fingering
- accurate articulation
- consistent rhythm

5. On most days when you practice this piece, begin on the second page and practice sections there first. Follow the same steps as above. Then go back to the first page. Return later to the second page so that it gets double practice.

6. When both pages are learned solidly so that no slips occur, work slowly to learn the entire piece. Gradually work it up to tempo, correcting all mistakes immediately.

7. Play the first two measures of each small section (measures 1-2, measures 9-10, measures 17-18, and measures 25-26) in a row. Aim to achieve different dynamic levels at each of these beginnings.

Finishing for performance

Ask yourself:

Does your legato sound smooth and even, without notes that are suddenly loud, punched, or too soft?

Do you hear the music flow so that it sounds like there is one pulse or beat in each measure?

Do you hear a different dynamic level at the beginning of each of the four smaller sections?

Do you hear a shape to each phrase?

Do you hear gentle endings to phrases?

If your answer is "no" to any of these questions, go back and practice to make the answer "yes," letting your ear be your guide.

To the Teacher

Affect: courtly, cheerful

Fingering: the most complicated shifts are in the right hand; student should learn the right hand alone solidly with correct fingering up to tempo

Number of ideas: this is longer than previous repertoire; more themes need to be worked out

Phrase definition: regular; 8 + 8 + 8 + 8; one large pulse for every two measures will help achieve the flow needed

Coordination: hands are quite independent; rhythmic working out of ornaments needs careful consideration from the beginning

This piece helps a student learn:
- coordination of independent voices
- fingering shifts
- control of legato and nuance in a phrase (the matching of tones)

Notes:
The familiarity of this selection makes it a favorite with students.

Classic Period

Priming for the Pinnacle

What is the pinnacle in playing Classic period music? Is it the ability to change the mood for each contrasting section or theme so that the music is alive? Is it the ability to play a beautiful singing melody over a soft, subdued but supporting accompaniment? Is it the ability to make the music elegant and refined? Is it the ability to phrase with finesse? The pinnacle includes all of these and more. We often hear music from the Classic period as background music in restaurants and other places. It is perfectly balanced music. It is elegant and refined music. It is music that soothes and calms us. Aim for the pinnacle by thinking about this and reading further about the special Classic sound.

Classic Music and the Use of Contrast

Baroque music generally featured one idea or affect through an entire piece. That idea helped the composer maintain consistency and unity in the piece. Composers in the Classic period reacted against this by trying to present different affections or feelings in a single work. In some of Mozart's most mature works, these changes occurred every few measures. In some sonatinas and sonatas of the Classic period, the second theme depicts a contrasting character or mood. This is followed with a section (the development section) where contrast occurs again.

In the Classic pieces found here, some will contain only one affect or mood. Other pieces will have a contrasting mood which is so strong that it needs a different affect. The first thing you should do with each piece is to read the melody and decide for yourself what the affect or affects are. What words could describe a section of the piece? Does it have several sections with strong contrast between them?

By doing this, your performance begins to come alive. The Classic period composers meant for the music to have contrast. They meant for the performer to find these different ideas and to communicate them through the way the music is played. You will enjoy looking for the mood or affect that you feel the composer wanted the melody to convey! Have fun!

Expression in Classic Music

Classic composers believed that attention to the small details was the secret of expression. Look for the small details to bring out and play expressively in your performance. You will find two-note slurs, appoggiaturas, and ornaments which make the melody more expressive. Also, you will find small articulation markings — staccatos, slurs, and other similar indications. These help create feeling and mood for Classic period composers. Be very careful to find all of the articulation markings which the composer wrote, so that your performance will be as true to the way he wanted it as possible.

Symmetry

Painting, sculpture, dance, poetry, and literature of the day displayed symmetry. Balance was of the utmost importance to all creative artists. Music also showed this symmetry, as you will easily hear.

Almost every aspect of Classic music was symmetrical. Short motives, phrases, even sections of pieces were often balanced with each other. If the music "asked" a question in a phrase, it was followed with a phrase or part of a phrase that "answered" the question. Often the rhythm was parallel in the symmetric sections. Look for as many instances of symmetry as you can find. You will eventually be able to predict what the music will sound like as a result of the symmetry.

Other Classic Period Traits

Music of this period at first seems to be simpler than Baroque music. The music of Baroque composers became so complex that the Classic period composers reacted against it. Their music is meant to sound simple and refined. That is one reason that symmetry and predictability are so much a part of this music.

Often in the Classic period you will hear a melody with an unadorned accompaniment. Most pieces in this volume have the melody in the right hand and a simple chordal accompaniment in the left hand. It is important to learn to play the accompaniment very softly so that the melody sings out. While in Baroque music two melodies often sound at the same time, the simpler Classic music features the singing melody over the accompaniment. Voicing the melody over accompaniment is an important consideration in playing Classic period literature.

Listen carefully to the flow of the phrase in Classic period pieces. This music is meant to be elegant — never harsh — and to flow and float. Listen for the goal of each phrase and make your phrase pull toward that note in a very smooth and suave way.

Listed for each piece are performance considerations which are emphasized in the selection

Waltz..Diabelli
- balance of melody and accompaniment
- flow of phrase
- aural awareness of phrase symmetry

Sonatina in C Major (Allegretto) .... Duncombe
- balance of melody and single-note accompaniment
- rhythm shifting from triplets to eighths
- movement about the keyboard

Sonatina in C Major (Moderato) .... Le Couppey
- balance of melody and Alberti accompaniment
- tonal control of phrase
- legato

Sonatina in C Major (Allegretto) .... Le Couppey
- balance of melody and single-note accompaniment
- facility in note-against-note playing
- detailed articulation

The Hunting Horns and Echo .... Türk
- finger crossings
- rhythmic precision
- interpretation of programmatic title
- facility in note-against-note playing

The Ballet .... Türk
- detailed articulation
- finger crossings
- voicing note-against-note

Bourlesq .... L. Mozart
- octave expansion
- changing fingers on same note
- rhythmic precision

Arietta in C Major .... Clementi
- detailed articulation
- balance of melody and single-note accompaniment
- playing two-note slurs

Sonatina in G Major (Allegro) .... Attwood
- balance of melody and Alberti accompaniment
- technical facility

Sonatina in C Major (Allegretto) .... Latour
- technical facility
- quick changes
- left hand extensions
- independence between the hands

Sonatina in G Major (Allegro) .... Latour
- balance of melody and Alberti accompaniment
- refinement in articulation
- rapid Alberti technique

Ecossaise in G Major WoO 23 .... Beethoven
- balance of melody and broken-chord accompaniment
- projection of humor in performance
- buoyancy of thick texture

Classic Literature

Waltz

Diabelli

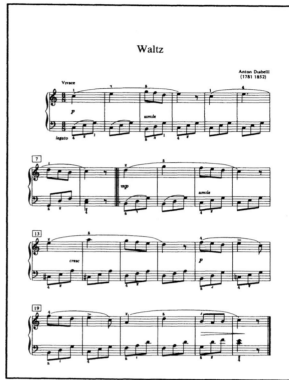

See *Masterwork Classics 3*, page 10.

Getting ready to play

(Write the answers in this book and on the music in Masterwork Classics.)

One of the first things that you observe is that Diabelli wants this piece played "vivace"—"lively." Since this piece is a waltz, be sure that your "lively" tempo does not become too fast to let your performance sound like a waltz.

Sight-read the right hand melody. What expressive mood (or "affect" or "affection") would you give the main theme? _____ Is there a new theme in this piece that needs another expressive mood? _____

Place brackets around the phrases of this piece. Which phrases were four measures long? _____ Which phrases were two measures long? _____ Were any phrases longer or shorter than two or four measures? _____

Notice the right hand rhythm of the first phrase. Write it here. _____ Which additional phrases use this exact rhythm in the right hand? _____ Are you surprised that the rhythm is exactly the same so often?! One characteristic of pieces in the Classic period is that there are many phrases which are "symmetric." This means that they balance each other and are similar in some way (such as length, rhythm, or patterns used). Another term we use which is comparable in meaning is "parallel."

Place an arrow above the treble staff over the note in each phrase which is the focal point. This is the note to which all other notes in the phrase seem to pull. It is the note to which you will gradually crescendo when playing each phrase. In which phrases do you have the arrow in the exact same place within the phrase? _____

Does the left hand play the melody at any time? _____ If not, you will want to play the left hand softly so that the melody projects above the left hand accompaniment.

Note the short slurs over the left hand like the one in measure 1. The slurs mean that you should play these notes grouped, without a break in sound.

What do you think will be the loudest note (or point) in this piece? _____ (*Hint:* Check the phrase that begins with measure 13 since this phrase has *cresc.* and the dynamic marking is the loudest in the piece.) What do you think will be the softest note or place in this piece? _____ (*Hint:* Find the place where the composer wrote a *dim.* and the dynamic level is *p*.)

Practicing for performance

(Answer the questions in your mind.)

Practice step by step. Be sure that you do not move on to the next step until you have met all of the thought and sound goals for the one before. These goals come from what you have learned about earlier pieces as well as what is written in the step. Your ear will tell you!

1. Practice the right hand alone for each phrase listening for and concentrating on
- correct fingering
- the affection you decided upon
- the focal point of each phrase
- a smooth legato with no punches or accents at the focal point
- gentle endings to each phrase
- a tempo slower than vivace
- symmetry of the rhythm between the phrases

You might make a game for yourself. Play right hand alone, perfectly (so that your ear tells you that it is right) six times in a row before you go to the next phrase.

2. Practice the left hand alone the same way you did the right hand in No. 1. Listen for the same points as you did above. Be certain that your fingering is exactly right!

3. Work on the first phrase, measures 1-4, hands together slowly at first and gradually work the phrase up to tempo. Listen to be sure you are meeting all of the goals under No. 1 before you move on to the next phrase. Once the two phrases in the first section are worked up to tempo, gradually increase the tempo of the entire first section to performance level. Listen to
- goals of phrases
- balance of melody and accompaniment
- the flow of your phrase (do you hear it flow or do you hear it note-by-note?)
- evenness of the notes in the left hand

4. Following the practice and listening steps in Nos. 1-3, work out the last section of the piece. Then, when this section is secure and played at a comfortable tempo that portrays the affect of this dance, combine both sections of the piece, listening for the same things as listed in No. 1. Here are some additional practice helps for both sections:

- To achieve the balance between hands so that the melody is louder than the accompaniment, feel the left hand play very lightly and play the right hand singing into the keys. To get this balance, you can practice the right hand *f* and the left hand *pp*. Then listen to the phrasing as you do that step again. If you still cannot achieve a light left hand, try feeling the first note of each measure with correct fingers at the base of the music rack of the piano. The right hand should feel the wood solidly and the left hand should be very light (even brush the wood).

- To achieve flowing phrases, count using one number per measure. Count 1 - 2 - 3 - 4. Begin the numbers over when you begin a new phrase. Listen to see if your piece sounds like there is one pulse per measure.

- Play two measures and then stop, and continue to the next measures in the following order and at these dynamic levels
  - *p* in measures 1-2
  - *mp* in measures 9-10
  - *p* in measures 17-18

to help your ear hear the different dynamic levels at the beginning of these sections. Practice until you hear a difference!

Finishing for performance

(Answer the questions in your mind.) Ask yourself:

Do you hear a smooth legato sound?

Do you hear the goal of every phrase?

Do you hear the left hand play more softly than the right hand which plays the melody?

Do you hear phrases that flow instead of ones that emphasize every note?

Do you hear the dynamics that are in the music?

Do you hear the note that is the climax of the entire piece?

Do you hear every phrase taper gently?

Do you hear every phrase begin gently without an accent?

Practice listening carefully to your playing until your answer to every question above is "yes."

To the Teacher

Affect: happy, jovial

Number of ideas: little to no contrast of themes; same mood throughout

Form: a buoyant dance in binary form

Balance: right hand melody over left hand broken-chord accompaniment

Symmetry: all phrases use the same rhythmic formula except measures 17-20 which are repetitions of two measures

Fingering: hands remain relatively close to C-major positions

Coordination: playing of melody and broken-chord accompaniment

This piece helps a student develop and hear:
- legato
- balance of melody above broken-chord accompaniment
- flow of a phrase
- aural awareness of phrase symmetry

Notes:

Pointing out the repeated rhythms in each phrase from the outset helps solidify the phrase symmetry and structure for the student.

The development of tonal control so that the line moves to a focal point is extremely important. This insures that the student gradually builds his/her skill and development of tonal control as the musical requirements in the literature increase.

Sonatina in C Major (Allegretto)   **Duncombe**

See *Masterwork Classics 3*, page 11.

Getting ready to play

Sight-read the melody in the right hand of this piece and listen to see whether the contrasts call for different affects. Or, will one affect fit the entire piece? _____ In what measure does the contrast begin? _____ In what measure does the main melody return? _____ Write here the dynamics for the first theme and for the contrasting theme. _____ What affect do you think fits the first theme? _____ If you have characterized a different mood or affect for the second theme, write it here. _____

Label each section of this piece with A or B. Where does the A section repeat? _____ Is the repetition exactly the same? _____

Write the rhythmic motive (the rhythm pattern) of measures 1-4. Indicate slurs that are in the score. _____
Write the rhythmic motive of measures 9-12 including the slurs.

_____

Notice that the dynamic indication in the bold A sections is *f*. The B section has two dynamic indications and a crescendo at the end, pulling the listener's ear back to the home music of the A section.

Bracket all phrases in the music. Were the phrases symmetrical as you expected? _____ You may have found longer phrases (four measures) in the A section and some shorter phrases in the B section (two measures). What earlier piece did the same thing? _____

Place an arrow at the point of greatest tension in each phrase. Your ear will help you know where that is. Hum or sing aloud with the melody each time you try to decide.

Practicing for performance

Practice step by step. Be sure that you do not move on to the next step until you have met all of the thought and sound goals for the one before. These goals come from what you have learned about earlier pieces as well as what is written in the step. Your ear will tell you!

1. Tap the rhythm for the first two measures, being very careful that your triplets are slow enough. Make the rhythm strong and bold the way the piece will sound. Try to give a feeling of one pulse per measure when you tap.

2. Play the right hand melody in this same rhythm for measures 1-4. Work to hear the phrase pull toward the focal point and check on your fingering. Then follow the same procedure for measures 5-8. Learn the left hand alone for measures 1-4 and then measures 5-8. Check fingering as you practice. Work on the first two phrases hands together. The second phrase will need more practice than the first (do you know why?). Work very slowly at first until you can play it correctly. Then increase the tempo slightly.

3. The melody in measures 9-14 repeats three times on different pitches. It is called a sequence. Practice this sequence, right hand alone. Can you memorize the pattern of the sequence by intervals? After playing the left hand alone for these six measures a couple of times, begin to work hands together on this sequence. First practice only measures 9-12. Then once you have learned this with correct fingering and the phrases pulling to the focal note, add measures 13-14.

4. When you practice measures 15-16, be sure you practice having no hesitations between measure 15 and measure 16 in the left hand. Keep the tempo steady. It is better to go very slowly and then to gradually increase the tempo.

5. Combine all of the phrases in the B section. If the cadence at measures 15-16 is still difficult to play, practice measures 13-16 thoroughly until your tempo is consistent and your fingering is correct. Now add the first part to it, measures 9-12 to measures 13-16. Listen carefully for
- a smooth legato with no suddenly loud or punched notes
- gently rounded phrases moving to the focal notes
- left hand accompaniment softer than the right hand
- dynamic differences as indicated in the score

6. Begin now to combine the A and B sections. It is better to take a sufficiently slow tempo that makes you able to listen and accomplish as much as possible. Any time before you play a passage fast in practice, you should play it slowly to refresh your mind, your fingers, and your ear. Listen for the same things as in No. 5 as you practice.

7. To achieve flow in your phrases, count 1 - 2 - 3 - 4 in the phrases in the A section using one number per measure. Do you hear which number that the phrase moves to? In the B section you could count to 8.

Finishing for performance

Ask yourself:

Do you hear the contrasting affections in your performance?

Do you hear the contrasting dynamics?

Do you hear a smooth legato sound (especially in the B section) with no punches or suddenly loud notes?

Do you hear the left hand accompaniment played softer than the right hand melody?

Do you hear the phrases taper gently?

Do you hear the crescendo in measures 15-16 signifying the return to the home or main theme?

At this point, practice so that you can answer "yes" to all of these questions letting your ear be the teacher.

To the Teacher

Affect: A section, bold; B section, sweet and gentle

Number of ideas: contrast of thematic material between the sections

Balance: right hand single-note melody above left hand single-note accompaniment

Phrase definition: regular

Fingering: left hand needs attention in measures 4-8

Coordination: difficult left hand skip in measures 15-16

This piece helps a student develop:
- solid rhythm shifting from triplets to eighths

  characterization of contrasting themes

Notes:

The student should continually practice to attain a balance between the hands as outlined in earlier pieces, since the voicing of melody over accompaniment is fundamental to this style.

Sonatina in C Major (Moderato)   Le Couppey

Sonatina in C Major

Felix Le Couppey
(1811 1887)

See *Masterwork Classics 3*, page 12.

Getting ready to play

This movement is marked moderato —"in a moderate tempo."
Play the right hand alone and decide on an affect or a mood for this
piece. _____

Which lines are exactly alike? _____

What is the dynamic marking for
line one? _____
line two? _____
line four? _____ (This has a different dynamic level
for each hand.)

Notice the dynamic marking in line three. Do you think the left
hand plays the melody in measures 17-20? _____Does the right
hand have the melody in measures 21-24? _____ Circle the same
melody notes in the right hand in measures 17-20 as you find in
measures 21-24.

Play the melody alone throughout the entire piece with correct
fingering.

How long is each phrase? _____ Mark each one with
brackets. Then put an arrow over the loudest note (magnet
note—note that draws the others to it) in each phrase. What measure of each phrase has the magnet note? _____ Keep this in
mind, because it will often be the same for other pieces from the
Classic period. This shows one reason why Classic period music is
"symmetrical."

Practicing for performance

Practice step by step. Be sure that you do not move on to the
next step until you have met all of the thought and sound goals for
the one before. These goals come from what you have learned
about earlier pieces as well as what is written in the step. Your ear
will tell you!

1. Practice measures 1-4 hands together, first slowly, then
gradually faster, until
• you play it phrased so that the magnet note pulls the
music to it
    • the phrase tapers at the end
    • the eighth notes sound smooth and even
    • all fingering is correct for each performance
    • you have no stumbles
    • the phrase reflects the mood

2. Do the same with
• measures 5-8
• measures 17-20
• measures 21-24

3. To achieve a balance with melody singing out over accompaniment, practice all three sections
  • slowly with the melody *f* and accompaniment *pp*
  • with melody slightly louder than the accompaniment (practice measures 17-20 extra)
  • playing melody aloud and playing accompaniment silently on top of the keys

4. Work on dynamics and balance of voices in the third line. Your ear will tell you when you are smooth and legato.

5. Work on the overall dynamics by playing measures 1-2, measures 9-10, measures 17-18, measures 21-22, and measures 25-26 in a row to hear the differences.

6. Play the entire piece slowly, then gradually faster. Listen for the same things as in practice step No. 1. Correct mistakes as you go. Gradually work it up to tempo.

Finishing for performance

Ask yourself:

Do you hear each phrase end gently?

Do you hear a gentle arch (rise and fall) in each phrase?

Do you hear the second phrase on each line answer the first phrase?

Do you hear the rhythm flow? Could your counting be 1 2 3 4 with one count in each measure for the first phrase? Try it for the other phrases.

Is your accompaniment very soft?

Practice listening carefully to your playing until your answer to every question above is "yes!"

To the Teacher

Affect: singing, carefree, pleasant (one affect throughout)

Form: A A B A

Balance: between hands, single-note melody and accompaniment

Symmetry: repetition of phrase A makes the rhythmic and melodic symmetry obvious

Fingering: generally remains close to C major five-finger position

Coordination: eighths against quarters

This piece helps a student develop:
  • balance of melody and accompaniment
  • control of tone in a phrase
  • legato
  • sense of phrasing

Notes:

The flow of this piece is enhanced if the student counts one pulse per measure.

The concept of symmetry in music of the Classic period (and other periods) can be heard easily in this selection with its repetition and predictable phrase lengths. All of the eight-measure phrases are comprised of question and answer patterns.

To further emphasize the aural understanding of symmetry in music of this period, the student should work to <u>hear</u> the movement within each phrase to the beginning of the third measure of the phrase.

Sonatina in C Major (Allegretto)   Le Couppey

See *Masterwork Classics 3*, page 12.

See *Masterwork Classics 3*, page 13.

Getting ready to play

Sight-read a portion of this movement and give it a word that describes the character or affect it should have. _____

Play the entire right hand melody with the correct fingering. As you play, circle any fingerings which you think may be difficult later.

Phrases in this piece are in four-measure groupings. Mark them with brackets.

Label each section of this piece with A or B. Since the last section is a shortened version of A, label it A'. Do you notice that all of the phrases in the A sections begin with the same short theme or motive? _____ Do you notice that the same thing happens in the B section? _____ Which measures might you call a "transition?" _____

Place arrows above the magnet note.

Write ♩♫|♩♩ in the music above the right hand at each occurrence of this rhythm or a slight variant of it. It is a kind of rhythmic motive that holds this piece together. Listen for it as you practice.

Practicing for performance

Practice step by step. Be sure that you do not move on to the next step until you have met all of the thought and sound goals for the one before. These goals come from what you have learned about earlier pieces as well as what is written in the step. Your ear will tell you!

1. Learn the right hand phrases separately listening for
   • smooth legato
   • the focal point and shape

2. Practice each of the four-measure phrases hands together. Listen for
   • smoothness of your sound
   • flowing phrases

3. To help achieve a desired balance between the melody and accompaniment,
   • practice right hand *f*, left hand ***p***
   • play on a table-top, making the left hand play so lightly that it brushes the top
   • play right hand as written, and play the left hand on top of the keys making no sound

4. Count each phrase using one number per measure (1 -2 -3 -4) for the entire piece. Which number gets the most emphasis each time? (Is it the third measure of each phrase?)

5. Play each section slowly hands together, gradually working it up to tempo.

6. Play the entire piece—all sections —slowly, gradually working it up to tempo.

Finishing for performance

Ask yourself:

Do you hear smooth and natural phrases?
Does the piece seem to flow?
Does your playing depict the character you decided upon?
Do you hear the phrases go to the focal points each time?
Do you hear gentle ends of phrases?
Do you hear the difference in the sections of this piece because the articulation in the middle section changes?
Do you hear the rhythmic motive tie it together?

Let your ear be your teacher as you practice to make all of your answers to these questions become "yes."

To the Teacher

Affect: cheerful

Balance: right hand single-note melody above left hand single-note accompaniment

Phrase definition: extremely regular

Symmetry: use of a single rhythmic idea with slight variation

Cadential pull: to the third measure in each four-measure phrase

Coordination: note-against-note

This piece helps a student develop:
• facility in note-against-note playing
• balance of melody and accompaniment

Notes:

The student should take his tempo from the left hand staccatos in measures 17-29. These should be played portato (as eighths) rather than very short.

Interest is generated from the chromaticism and four-measure extension in measures 33-37. The non-symmetry of this one phrase draws our attention to it since it is non-predictable.

Using two pianos, the concept of dialogue (or the question and answer phrasing) can be demonstrated by having the teacher play the first two measures of each group and the student respond by playing the last two measures in tempo. In the B section, four-measure groups rather than two-measure groups can alternate between teacher and student. The roles may be reversed in this activity.

The Hunting Horns and Echo   Türk

See *Masterwork Classics 3*, page 14.

Getting ready to play

This title is "programmatic." That is, it tells the performer something about the story or scene reflected in the music. This piece might portray the sound of hunting horns with an echo. Glancing at the music, we notice a *f* section, then *pp*, then a *f* section, and then *pp*. The *f* could represent the horns and the *pp* the echo.

Music of the Classic period is made of contrasts. This piece demonstrates those contrasts. Affects for this piece might be the "sound of nearby horns" contrasting with "echo of horns."

Do the right hand and left hand follow the same rhythm throughout the whole piece? _____ Tap out the rhythm of the right hand in measures 1-5. Tap it several times, first in slow tempo and later increasing the pace slightly. How is the rhythm for the B section different from that of the A section? _____

Sight-read the right hand in the first half of the piece and write in any additional fingerings you need to play this piece well. Do the same for the left hand of the A section and the B section.

How long is the first phrase? _____ Mark it with brackets. The first part of the piece sounds like a four-measure phrase with one measure added at the end for the echo. The same thing happens for the B section. You could say the phrase outline is 4 + 1 + 4 + 1.

Place an arrow above the focal point of all of the phrases. One of several answers could be correct. One correct answer might put the focal point at the first note of the third measure. Has this happened before? _____

Practicing for performance

Practice step by step. Be sure that you do not move on to the next step until you have met all of the thought and sound goals for the one before. These goals come from what you have learned about earlier pieces as well as what is written in the step. Your ear will tell you!

1. Play the right hand alone in the A section
   • slowly
   • counting carefully
   • with correct fingering
until you have achieved all of these each time. Then increase the tempo until you are playing the right hand alone
   • up to tempo
   • achieving correct rhythm
   • with correct fingering
   • shaping so that you hear the focal note

2. Follow the same procedure in practicing the left hand of the A section.

3. Practice the A section hands together thinking about and listening for
- exact rhythm
- correct fingering in both hands
- steady tempo
- phrasing which pulls to the focal point

Work very slowly, then gradually faster.

4. Follow the same procedure for the B section as you did for the A section in Nos. 1-3 above.

5. Additional practice pointers to help you are the following:
- listen for your phrases to flow—you can do this by counting 1 - 2 in each measure, not 1 - 2 - 3 - 4
- listen to make the half notes in measures 4, 5, 9, 10 end at exactly the right time and the silence begin at the right time

Finishing for performance

Ask yourself:

Do you hear echoes?
Do you hear strong steady rhythm?
Do you hear phrases pull to the peaks?
Do your phrases flow so that they have two beats per measure?

Let your ear be your teacher as you practice to make all of your answers to these questions "yes."

To the Teacher

Affect(s): bold theme contrasted by *pp* echo; contrast of affections within section—a rudimentary reference to the concept of "contrast" of themes or ideas which is a prevalent characteristic of Classic music

Balance: right hand single-note melody above left hand single-note accompaniment

Phrase definition: 4 + 1 + 4 + 1

Symmetry: both halves are parallel in rhythm and phrase structure

Cadential pull: to the third measure of each phrase

Fingering: crossings in both hands at different times; needs attention

Coordination: finger crossings not simultaneous between hands

This piece helps a student develop:
- finger crossings
- rhythmic precision
- interpretation of programmatic title

Notes:
Fingering accuracy must be worked out in the initial learning stages. Crossings at non-simultaneous times are difficult.

Student and teacher could play this at two pianos in a similar manner to the "allegretto" from the Le Couppey Sonatina. The teacher might play the *f* phrase and the student answer with the echo. The roles may be reversed. This helps the student hear the dialogue in the music and count the long silences.

The tempo should be "moderato" rather than very slow as some students will want to play.

The Ballet

Türk

The Ballet

Allegro non tanto

D G Türk
(1756 1813)

See *Masterwork Classics 3*, page 15.

Getting ready to play

The title of this piece is a programmatic one. That is, it already tells us something about the story of this piece. What Classic piece did you study earlier that also had a programmatic title? _____

Sight-read the right hand melody to listen for contrast. The part before the repeat seems to sound as if the dancer may be dancing "delicately on toe." The sixteenth notes contrast by sounding as if the dancer may be "twirling around and around." These can be the affects for this piece.

What is the form? _____ Are you surprised by the number of measures in the A and B sections? _____ These parallel phrases reflect what aspect of Classic period music that you have observed again and again? _____

Place brackets around the phrases. Then place arrows in each at the focal point of the phrase.

Since symmetry and repetition occur so frequently in the Classic period, look for occurrences of repetition in this piece. The last four measures, measures 13-16 are similar to which other measures? _____ Circle the difference in both cases. Which other motive is repeated in this piece? _____

The indication "non legato" found at the beginning of this piece indicates that you should play slightly detached. Use the half-staccato or portato touch that you learned while playing Baroque period music.

You will notice that the section with the contrasting affect (measures 9-12) is played legato and that the note values are faster there than in the other sections. This is the way that the composer creates the different mood.

Practicing for performance

Practice step by step. Be sure that you do not move on to the next step until you have met all of the thought and sound goals for the one before. These goals come from what you have learned about earlier pieces as well as what is written in the step. Your ear will tell you!

1. Write in any fingerings for the right hand on line two that you feel you will need to help you follow the fingering plan already written into your music.

2. Learn the right hand alone in measures 1-4 aiming for correct fingering and hearing the focal point of the phrase. Then add the left hand after practicing it alone several times. Be sure that the fingering is absolutely correct.

3. Follow the same procedure in working out measures 5-8 and then measures 13-16.

4. Combine both phrases in the A section. Listen for the following in your playing
- light portatos
- phrases pulling to the focal note
- light left hand accompaniment
- even sixteenth notes

5. Learn the right hand in the contrasting section, measures 9-12. Listen to hear the extreme dynamic contrast. Then combine both hands in this section, listening for dynamic contrast from both hands!

6. Combine both parts in the B section listening for the same things as in No. 4 above.

7. Work on the piece as a whole, combining all of the sections. If you have special trouble with one of the phrases, take it alone and practice it separately until you have reached your sound goal. Listen for the goals that are listed in No. 4 above.

Finishing for performance

Ask yourself:

Do you hear light, buoyant staccatos?

Do your phrases have one pulse per measure rather than two or four?

Does your playing reflect the two different affects that the title and the music seem to be calling for ("dancing on toes" and then "twirling around and around")?

Do you hear dynamic contrasts when you repeat the A section and in the "twirls" in the B section?

Do you hear focal points of your phrases?

Do you hear a light left hand accompaniment?

Practice with these sound goals in mind letting your ear be your teacher until you can answer "yes" to all of these questions.

To the Teacher

Affects: dancing on toes, then twirling around

Number of ideas: two distinct contrasting ideas; they need different characterizations

Balance: right hand single-note melody above left hand single-note accompaniment

Phrase definition: extremely regular

Fingering: right hand crossings on line one need attention

This piece helps a student develop:
- finger crossings
- portrayal of contrasting themes

Bourlesq   L. Mozart

See *Masterwork Classics 3*, page 16

Getting ready to play

The editor has given an affect for this piece—"happily." A "bourlesq" or "burlesque" is a light and humorous piece or a musical farce. Sight-read through the right hand melody. If you think of another affect that fits this piece and is similar to "happily," write it here. _____

Label measures 1-4 <u>a</u> (not a capital A because this section is too short to be a major section). Subsection <u>a</u> repeats. The part after <u>a</u> looks as if it could be called <u>b</u> since it is different. This section is five measures long. You notice that <u>a</u> repeats again. The plan of this piece is probably <u>a</u> <u>a</u> <u>b</u> <u>a</u>. Do you agree? _____ Label these sections in your music.

Place an arrow at the focal point of each phrase.

The dynamic plan for this piece is:

<u>a</u>	*f*
<u>a</u>	*p*
<u>b</u>	*f* and *p*
<u>a</u>	*f*

Do you understand how the music shows you that plan? _____

What interval does the left hand use throughout this piece? _____ Is it broken or blocked? _____

Practicing for performance

Practice step by step. Be sure that you do not move on to the next step until you have met all of the thought and sound goals for the one before. These goals come from what you have learned about earlier pieces as well as what is written in the step. Your ear will tell you!

1. Learn the right hand alone in the <u>a</u> section. Listen and check for:
   • correct fingering
   • articulation
   • peaks of phrases

2. Look at the score and say the name of the first note of each left hand octave. Can you almost memorize this pattern? Now play the left hand skeleton—the first note of each octave as a quarter note—with your fifth finger on each note. Now play the left hand octaves (both notes) in the <u>a</u> section.

3. Very slowly, learn the A section hands together. Keep moving your tempo slower until you make no mistakes and are correct in rhythm, phrasing, and articulation. Once you accomplish the goals of No. 1 with both hands, move the tempo up just a bit. When you first start to learn this piece hands together, the coordination will seem difficult. The trick is to play very slowly to be exactly right. It is like trying to pat your head and rub your stomach! Think about how you would learn to do that. (Slowly at first!)

4. Follow the same procedure for learning the b section that you did with the a section above in Nos. 1-3. Be sure you contrast your dynamics!

5. Combine all of the sections of this piece. Listen carefully to be sure you are accomplishing the goals above and that your tempo is consistent. Also, listen to hear the dynamic plan of the entire piece that was outlined above. Remember, it is not unusual for this to be difficult at first. Be very careful to play correctly at a slow tempo. Then increase the tempo just a bit. Soon you will have it up to tempo.

Finishing for performance

Ask yourself:

Do you hear this piece sound "happy" and whatever additional affect you decided upon?

Do you hear the dynamic plan that was indicated in your music and that you outlined above?

Do you hear the magnet note of each phrase?

Do you hear the left hand accompaniment soft and the right hand melody sing out over the accompaniment?

Do you hear buoyant, light staccatos?

Do you hear the first note of each octave emphasized more than the second note?

Does your performance of the "Bourlesq" sound like a light and humorous composition?

Let your ear be the teacher as you practice so that you are able to answer "yes" to all of these questions.

To the Teacher

Affect: happy, carefree

Balance: right hand melody above left hand broken-octave accompaniment

Phrase definition: phrases in b section are two and one-half measures each, but the sound is regular and symmetrical

Fingering: 5 - 1 on left hand octaves

Coordination: motor skills required are more difficult than before

This piece helps a student develop:
- changing fingers on the same note
- rhythmic precision
- a feeling for the left hand octave span

Notes:
The sixteenth-note activity in the right hand will help develop technical facility.

Arietta in C Major

Clementi

See *Masterwork Classics 3*, page 17.

Getting ready to play

This piece is marked "allegretto." Sight-read the right hand melody to listen for contrast. Do you think that there is one affect or mood for this piece? _____ Or do you find a place where it seems to contrast slightly? _____ If so, mark the measure numbers that contrast. _____

What is the primary affect or expressive mood of the piece? _____ If you feel that the third line could have a slightly different mood, what would be the expressive quality for these four measures? _____

Place brackets around the phrases in this piece. Did you find any phrases that were not four measures long? _____

Hum or sing as you read the melody again. Place an arrow at the magnet note of each phrase.

Does the left hand ever play the melody? _____

Compare the right hand rhythm in lines one, two, four, and five. Write the rhythm for each line here.

_____ line one
_____ line two
_____ line four
_____ line five

Notice how close the rhythmic patterns are to each other. The first two measures of each phrase are practically alike! This helps show the symmetry of this piece. Do you also notice that all of the phrases are the same length? _____ Both the rhythm and the phrase structure are very symmetrical in "Arietta."

In Classic period music, composers ask the performer to be very expressive in some special cases:

(1) in playing appoggiaturas
(2) in playing other two-note slurs

Appoggiaturas are a special kind of two-note slur. An appoggiatura is a stressed note for which your ear is not prepared. It is a surprise and often even sounds wrong at first. You should emphasize the appoggiatura—lean on the first note and make the second one taper gently. Doing this makes the music expressive. "Arietta" has an appoggiatura in measure 16. Circle the note that sounds "tense"—the note that you will lean on.

Two-note slurs are treated in exactly the same way. You will lean on the first note and gently taper the second note.

Circle the first note of the two-note slurs in measures 2, 4, 6, 12, 15. Are you surprised at how many "tense" notes there are to lean on? _____ This is an important part of Classic period music. You will be surprised to find many of these in other pieces too!

Practicing for performance

Practice step by step. Be sure that you do not move on to the next step until you have met all of the thought and sound goals for each step. These goals come from what you have learned about earlier pieces as well as what is written in the step. Your ear will tell you!

1. Practice line one and then line two, hands together, listening for and checking on
- correct fingering
- smooth phrases that pull to the peak
- graceful two-note slurs that lean on the first note
- tapering at the end of phrases

2. Lines four and five are similar, but they appear to be more difficult. Therefore, first practice hands separately listening for the same goals as in No. 1. Then learn each phrase hands separately, still listening carefully. Finally, learn the two phrases hands together. Notice that the dynamic level changes strongly on the last line!

3. The third line might have a different emotion or affect. Think about playing this line more strongly. It does not seem quite as graceful as the other sections.

4. Practice connecting lines three, four, and five. Listen carefully and work until you can play these three lines up to tempo, listening for
- correct moods and affects
- dynamic change on line five
- pull of the phrases to the focal point
- leaning on and then tapering of two-note slurs

5. Now follow the same procedure as in No. 4 with the entire piece—joining both parts.

6. Some additional practice hints:
- If you are practicing a section and following these steps, and you cannot make the phrase sound the way your ear tells you it should, reduce the tempo substantially and listen carefully. Continue to slow the tempo until you are able to accomplish your goals.
- Practice carefully to hear the right hand melody louder than the left hand accompaniment. Keep the left hand very soft. A way to practice keeping the left hand soft, in addition to the way we discussed in the last lesson, is to play the right hand as usual while shadow-playing the left hand on top of the keys (do not let the keys go down).

Finishing for performance

Ask yourself:

Do you hear smooth legato phrasing?

When you lean on the first note of an appoggiatura or two-note slur, do you hear a gentle lean rather than a heavy accent?

Do your phrases flow so that you hear two pulses per measure?

Do you play so that you hear the symmetry of the phrases?

Do you hear music pull to the focal point of each phrase?

Does your performance match the affects you decided on?

Practice listening carefully to your playing until your answer to every question above is "yes."

To the Teacher

Affect: singing; the third line contains contrasting material but probably does not need a different affect here

Balance: right hand single-note melody above left hand single-note accompaniment

Symmetry: phrases and rhythmic structure are symmetric between lines one, two, four, and five

Fingering: set positions except the left hand crossings in line five

This piece helps a student develop:
- playing of two-note slurs
- balance of melody and accompaniment
- Classic phrasing

Notes:

It is helpful for the student to sing or hum the melody to help encourage shaping of the phrases.

The phrase flow and shape should be worked out and heard in the left hand as well as the right hand. Once the student hears shape in the lower part, he begins to listen to the polarity of voices in a performance.

Sonatina in G Major (Allegro)

See *Masterwork Classics 3*, page 18.

See *Masterwork Classics 3*, page 19.

Getting ready to play

This piece is marked "allegro," "happy." Sight-read the right hand of this piece and decide whether you think the same affect will work for the entire piece or whether your ear hears contrast. (<u>Hint:</u> The dynamic change and the different kinds of right hand and left hand figures in measure 9 might give you a clue.) What affect do you think the first section (*f* and *mf*) should have? _____ What affect do you feel the second section (*p*) should have? _____

Sight-read the melody again to help divide this piece into sections. Look for two things right now:

    (1) a place where the main theme repeats

    (2) a place where the rhythmic motive (pattern) of the melody or the accompaniment changes

Which measures will you include in the A section? _____ Which measures are in the B section? _____ Which measures are in the return of the A section? _____

In looking at the symmetry of this piece, you have already noticed that the A section repeats. Does any part of the B section repeat? _____ Notice how the left hand is different in this repetition.

Place brackets around the phrases here. Then place an arrow over the focal note in each phrase.

Only one phrase in this piece is not symmetrical. What are the measure numbers? _____ This unusual phrase was put in by the composer to be humorous and to serve as a bridge to the return of the A section. It is a kind of joke in music since

    (1) the left hand stops playing

    (2) the right hand repeats the first motive three times as if the listener missed it

    (3) the right hand repeats D and C-sharp over and over so that the listener does not know when it will end

    (4) the phrase is an irregular length and ends at an unusual time

Think about what you will do to play this like a joke when you get to it in the music.

The left hand broken-chord pattern in measures 1-4 and other places is called an "Alberti bass" when it is broken in this way The "Alberti bass" is a common accompaniment pattern for Classic period pieces. Hearing an Alberti bass signals to you that the piece probably is from this period. Remember to watch for this in other pieces too.

Practicing for performance

Practice step by step. Be sure that you do not move on to the next step until you have met the thought and sound goals for the one before. These goals come from what you have learned about earlier pieces as well as what is written here. Your ear will tell you!

1. To learn the left hand Alberti bass, first play the left hand as blocked chords in measures 1-6. (Simultaneously play all three notes of the chord.) In 4/4 time, play a chord on beats 1 and 3 and use the other beats to find the next chord. Be sure you play the chords with the exact fingering that you will use in playing the original Alberti bass.

2. Play the Alberti bass as written in measures 1-6 Try to keep your thumb very quiet. The thumb is the strongest finger and will have a tendency to be loud. Play it very lightly just as you learned earlier to voice the entire left hand down and play softly.

3. Tap out the rhythm of measures 1-4. Listen for peaks of phrases and be very careful with fingering. Once this is mastered, continue by learning the right hand part for measures 5-8 The fingering here is especially tricky. After you have learned the right hand well for these 8 measures, practice the right hand alone alternating measure 4 and measures 7-8. This will help you be very solid later.

4. Learn measures 1-4 hands together. Concentrate on and listen carefully for
- correct fingering
- legato sound
- smooth Alberti with quiet thumb
- left hand softer than right hand melody
- smooth rhythm when the ornament is played
- goals of the phrases

You will want to practice very slowly to do this. Once you can play slowly accomplishing these goals, continue by practicing slightly faster, making sure you still hear these goals being met.

5. Follow the same procedure for learning measures 5-8. Then, once both sections are up to tempo and you hear all of the goals, combine the two sections.

6. In the B section, learn the right hand alone for measures 8-12. (The right hand is the same for measures 13-16.) Then learn the left hand alone for measures 8-12 and measures 13-16.

7. When you combine the left hand and right hand in the B section, measures 13-16 will be more difficult than the first part. Practice this part very slowly. Once you can play it perfectly slowly about five times in a row meeting all of the sound goals from above, begin to practice measures 9-12. Work here in the same way, then combine both phrases. Listen attentively with the sound goals in mind and be absolutely sure that rhythm and fingering are correct.

8. Learn the humorous part, measures 17-19, and then connect it to the earlier part of the B section. Measures 17-19 are a bridge to the return of the A section.

9. Combine the B section and the last A section of the piece. Any time you hear a phrase that does not meet with your original sound goal, work hard on that place before playing a longer portion. Once these two sections are learned well, you can add the first A section to it. By practicing this part in the order B A and then A B A, you practice the more difficult B section first, giving it the most alert practice. Be sure that you are listening for:
- phrases that flow with two pulses per measure
- left hand accompaniment that is softer than the melody
- the different dynamics in the piece
- contrasting affections or moods of the sections
- smooth legato and singing tone
- phrases that gently taper

Finishing for performance

Ask yourself:

Do you hear the phrases flow in your playing?

Do you hear the contrast of affects?

Do you hear the dynamics in the music?

Do you hear a light Alberti bass (and light thumb)?

Does the last phrase (the short one) in the B section make you laugh?

Does the ornament sound smooth and fit into the rhythm?

Practice letting your ear be your teacher so that you can answer "yes" to all of these questions.

To the Teacher

Affects: section A, strolling; section B, whimsical

Number of ideas: contrast of thematic material in B to that in A

Balance: right hand single-note melody above left hand Alberti and other accompaniments

Phrase structure: extremely regular; the one three-measure phrase is easily heard as humor

Fingering: some left hand extensions

Coordination: ranges from short note values in right hand against moving left hand to quicker right hand note values against longer left hand values; this contrast and reversal needs attention.

This piece helps a student develop:
- coordination of fast against slow note values and, in the same piece, slow against fast note values
- Alberti bass technique
- balance of melody against a fast-moving accompaniment

Notes:

The student may need to devote considerable time to working on the balance of melody and accompaniment in this piece. The balance requirements are more advanced than before.

Sonatina in C Major (Allegretto)   Latour

See *Masterwork Classics 3*, page 20.

See *Masterwork Classics 3*, page 21.

Getting ready to play

Play the right hand melody of the entire piece to help determine if the piece shows one affect or two affects. In the second part, beginning with measure 9, the slurs over groups of notes are short. The slurs in the first part were very long. Is this contrast in slurring strong enough to need a different affect from the original one in the piece? _____ What affect did you decide upon for this piece? _____ If you have a different affect for the contrasting theme, what is it? _____

Where does the melody of the first theme return toward the end of this piece? _____ How long does it remain the same as at the beginning of the piece? _____ Does this piece also have a very short ending section that one might call a codetta? _____

Before you finish discovering the form, bracket the phrases. (Your phrases could be 2 or 4 measures in some cases.) Place an arrow at the peak of each phrase.

In discovering the form, you notice that the repeat sign could indicate the end of a section. Where does the A section end? _____ Which measures are in the B section? _____ Circle the notes in the return of the A section that are different from the first A section. Measures 26–27 with upbeats can be called a codetta. This area can also be included as part of the final A section.

Do you notice that all of the phrases in this piece seem to ask a question and then have an answer? _____ Sight-read the melody listening for that. That is another aspect of symmetry in Classic period pieces.

Look for all of the repetitions of melody that you can find in this piece.

     measures 1–2 repeat in _____, _____, _____, _____
     measure 3 repeats in _____, _____, _____, _____
     measure 9 repeats in _____, _____, _____
     measure 10 repeats in _____

Each phrase in the B section begins the same but the endings sometimes are different. Circle the three different endings used in these four phrases.

Write the dynamic plan for this piece.

measures 1–4	_____	A
measures 5–8	_____	
measures 9–16	_____	B
measures 17–20	_____	A
measures 21–25	_____	
measures 26–27	_____	Codetta

What kind of scale do you find in measure 1? _____

Notice the fermata in measure 16. In the time that this was written, a cadenza may have been improvised. The cadenza gave the performer the opportunity to "show off." You may play the cadenza written at the bottom of the page, or you may improvise your own cadenza.

Practicing for performance

Practice step by step. Be sure that you do not move on to the next step until you have met the thought and sound goals for the one before. These goals come from what you have learned about earlier pieces as well as what is written here. Your ear will tell you!

1. Learn the right hand alone for measures 1–4 and measures 5–8. Concentrate on achieving correct fingering and listen for a smooth legato and to hear peaks of phrases. Practice the left hand alone for measures 1–8 concentrating and listening in the same way.

2. Learn measures 1–4 and then measures 5–8 hands together. Listen for and check on
- fingering
- legato sound
- rise and fall of phrase to the peak
- two pulses per measure
- dynamic contrast between the phrases

3. Work on the end of the final A section and the codetta. Begin in measure 24 and work hands separately at first. Listen for the same goals as in No. 2 above.

4. Combine the final A section and the codetta working toward the same goals as in No. 2. Learn this ending so that you can play without hesitations and stumbles. Make it sound strong at the end but not heavy. Can you make a difference in your playing between heavy and loud?

5. You may need to practice the B section hands alone. If you find that you do, work in groups of two measures. Continue by working out measures 9–10 hands together, slowly at first. Then, after you have accomplished the sound goals listed above, gradually increase your tempo until you can play up to tempo with the sound and fingering goals met. Do the same thing for measures 11–12. Then combine these four measures.

6. All notes in measures 13–16 are the same as before except for a couple of notes in measure 16. Check on these and combine both parts of section B. Aim for no stops and for consistency in sound. This section has shorter phrases than the A section. Practice to be sure that you can hear these short phrases the way the slurs in the music indicate.

7. Learn the cadenza at the bottom of this page. Or, compose one yourself. (The cadenza could also be omitted.)

8. Combine the cadenza with the B section.

9. Practice now from the B section to the end. If you find places where you do not sound solid or do not meet your sound goals, take them out and work on them. This should happen each time you play it.

10. When you have learned well the portion from B to the end, add the A section. Keep listening for legato and smooth, flowing phrases.

Finishing for performance

Ask yourself:

Does your performance reflect the affect (or affects) you decided upon?

Do you hear smooth phrases and legato sound without punched notes?

Does your playing flow with one or two pulses per measure?

Do you hear the dynamic plan you wrote out above?

Do you hear how the short phrases in the B section contrast with the longer ones in the A sections?

Do you hear a soft left hand accompaniment that lets the right hand sing out above it?

Let the goal of your practice now be to answer "yes" to each of these questions. These questions will give you the sound goals for which to strive.

To the Teacher

Affect: playful

Number of ideas: the contrasting theme in the B section has essentially the same character as the first theme; however, these short phrases contrast with the longer phrases in A

Form: this is the first piece which approaches sonata form; it is still analyzed as "A B A Codetta" since the material in the B section is new rather than developmental and there is no second theme in the A section

Phrase definition: extremely regular; student should hear the short phrases of the B section in contrast to the long phrases in the A section

Coordination: B section requires quick changes from right hand eighths above quarter notes to right hand quarter notes above eighths

This piece helps a student develop:
- quick changes in coordination
- facility in faster passagework
- left hand extensions
- smooth and even legato sound

Notes:

The student will need to work with the B section slowly to coordinate the alternating eighths and quarters between hands.

This piece provides a good opportunity for the student to work on evenness of sound in playing scale passages, especially the absence of thumb bumps.

Chords in measures 24–27 should be played buoyantly, never in a heavy manner.

It is difficult to determine whether the contrast in this piece is sufficiently substantial to require the verbalization of contrasting affects. The teacher or student may define one mood to continue throughout, or may define two affects for contrast of thematic character.

The insertion of a cadenza in measure 16 is optional, but is recommended.

Sonatina in G Major (Allegro)   **Latour**

See *Masterwork Classics 3*, page 22.

See *Masterwork Classics 3*, page 23.

Getting ready to play

This piece, like many first movements of sonatinas and sonatas, is marked "allegro," "happy." Sight-read the right hand melody and decide whether you feel that one affect holds for the entire piece or whether you hear contrast and need two affects. The contrasting theme is marked *p* and the first theme was *mf* and *f*. This second theme does contrast, but the change is more in dynamics than a change of character. One affect will be appropriate for the entire piece. Write that affect here. _____

Since this piece is longer than some earlier pieces, divide it into phrases before you find the form. That will help in determining the form. Place brackets around each phrase. Are the phrase lengths predictable? _____ What are the measure numbers of the one unpredictable phrase? _____ How is it similar to the humorous measures that appeared just before the return of the A section in the Attwood sonatina? _____

Where does the main theme return in this piece? _____ How many measures are like the beginning section? _____ Label the A section and the return of the A section. Measures 9-19 comprise the B section. The dynamics contrast with those before and the theme here is a new one. The form through measure 28 is A B A. The last measures at the end are a kind of short ending to round off the piece. Often sonatinas have short endings such as this, called "codettas." Label measures 28-end "codetta." The form of this sonatina is similar to the last one you played. The material at the end of both B sections does two things.

(1) leads back to the main theme and
(2) repeats the same notes and harmony several times.
This section could be called a "bridge."

Place an arrow over the point of greatest tension in each phrase.

What is the dynamic plan of each phrase in this piece?

A section	_____	phrase one
	_____	phrase two
B section	_____	phrase one
	_____	phrase two
	_____	phrase three (bridge)
A section	_____	phrase one
	_____	phrase two
Codetta	_____	

What is the name of the kind of left hand accompaniment in measure 1? (*Hint:* You played the same kind of accompaniment in the last sonatina.) _____

Are there any measures with eighth notes in the left hand that do not use this special kind of accompaniment? _____

Circle two-note slurs in this piece (right hand). Did you find them in measures 1, 3, 4, 5, 10, 12, 14, 20, 22, 23, 24, 29? _____ Remember that when you play, you will lean gently on the first note and taper the second.

Practicing for performance

Practice step by step. Be sure that you do not move on to the next step until you have met the thought and sound goals for the one before. These goals come from what you have learned about earlier pieces as well as what is written here. Your ear will tell you!

1. Practice the left hand Alberti bass exactly the same way you did in the last sonatina by Attwood. Play the left hand first as blocked chords—that is, play the first three notes of each measure together as a chord. Do this in the rhythm of the piece—2/4—playing the chord on beats 1 and 2 and using the "ands" to find the next chord. Since the chords do not change often in this piece, you might want to take out measures with chord changes in them like measures 3, measures 9-10, measures 26-29 and practice them alone to learn the chord change.

2. As you did in the previous piece, now play the left hand Alberti bass as written. Remember to keep your thumb very light. You might practice letting your thumb barely play. Measures 24-32 will need the most practice. Practice this part first and continue to sandwich it into your practice so that it gets plenty of extra practice.

3. Learn the right hand alone for measures 1-8. Practicing it alone gives you a chance to be especially careful with the fingering, articulation and two-note slurs, and the shape of the phrase.

4. Combine both hands for the A section. Work very slowly at first. Play at a tempo at which you can hear the right hand articulation and two-note slurs, the quiet left hand, a consistent rhythm, and the accomplishment of the goals of the section. Once this is easy to play and you meet your sound goals, gradually work the tempo up just a bit faster until you can play each section alone almost up to tempo.

5. Practice the return of the A section near the end. Measure 26 contains different material. Be sure you learn this well.

6. Review the left hand Alberti bass for the B section. You might find it helpful to practice both Nos. 1 and 2 again for this section.

7. Learn the right hand alone for the B section with the same goals as in No. 3 above.

8. Combine both hands for the B section, listening for the same goals and practicing as you did in No. 4 above.

9. Practice the codetta, measures 28-32, in the same way. Notice that the motive in measure 28 repeats in measure 30—so practice it alone before combining both motives.

10. As you did when practicing the Attwood sonatina, combine the B section and the last A section of the piece. Once these two sections are learned well, add the codetta. Your final step will be to add the first A section so that you are playing A B A Codetta. Be sure that you are meeting the sound goals that you know to listen for. Be especially careful that your phrases flow—that they move forward gently with one pulse per measure and that your playing is not too heavy.

Finishing for performance

Ask yourself:

Do you hear goals of your phrases?
Do you hear the articulation?
Do the two-note slurs lean on the first note and then gently taper?
Does the Alberti bass stay quietly in the background?
Do you hear the dynamic plan of the piece written in the music?
Are the staccatos light?

Focus your practice now so that your goal is to answer "yes" to every question.

To the Teacher

Affect: carefree

Number of ideas: second theme contrast comes more from a dynamic nuance than from change of character

Balance: right hand single-note melody above left hand Alberti bass

Phrase definition: regular; phrases may be heard as two-measure phrases or as four-measure phrases

Fingering: only several shifts

Coordination: left hand Alberti needs facility; coordination of both hands playing note-against-note could be difficult in those passages

This piece helps a student develop:
• rapid Alberti bass technique
• coordination of rapid note-against-note passages between the hands
• refinement in articulation

Notes:
The tempo should not be a slow one. Students will need to consider facility, flexibility, and speed in playing the Alberti bass. Some of the hands-together playing here is rapid and needs fine coordination.

Students still need to continue working on balance of melody and accompaniment. That is particularly appropriate and necessary for this section since a light and rapid left hand is difficult to achieve.

Ecossaise in G Major, WoO 23 **Beethoven**

See *Masterwork Classics 3*, page 24.

Getting ready to play

Beethoven marked this piece "allegro," "happy." Sight-read the melody in the right hand. Do you find contrast that needs a different affect from the opening one? Or will one affect go all the way through? _____ What is that affect? _____

This piece looks like it might be in binary form since there are eight measures in the first section and eight in the second section. Notice the "D.C. al Fine" at the end of measure 16! This piece is in A B A form. You should repeat the first A and B sections but not the last A section. Thus, in the final performance you should play it in this order: A A B B A.

Several places in the piece let us know that this is meant to be a humorous or funny piece. Notice the sudden leap upward in measures 2 and 6 in the right hand! Then notice the unexpected A-sharp in the right hand in measure 4! Lean on these notes slightly when you play them. Also, find the accent markings in measures 13 and 14. They come on a syncopated beat. Again, Beethoven is trying to be humorous in throwing us off of the strong beat! Remember to play slight accents here. Finally, after the loud and humorous events in measures 9-14, the music suddenly becomes *p*. This suddenly *p* place should be another humorous event.

Place arrows at the focal point of each phrase. In some cases, do you think it should be the "humorous" note? _____

Some of the ideas repeat in this piece. Measures 1-4 are repeated almost exactly in which measures? _____ Measures 9-10 are repeated almost exactly in which measures? _____

Which line uses only broken octaves in the left hand? _____ Which piece have you recently learned that also had left hand broken octaves? _____

Practicing for performance

Practice step by step. Be sure that you do not move on to the next step until you have met all of the thought and sound goals for the one before. These goals come from what you have learned about earlier pieces as well as what is written in the step. Your ear will tell you!

1. Look at the left hand broken chords in lines one and two. Circle the only two measures that are different between the lines. Practice the left hand as blocked chords first. Learn it this way, left hand only, in 2/4 time, playing the chord on the first eighth of each measure. Be sure your counting is steady and slow. The last three eighth-rests in the measure give you time to find the next chord. Set a tempo that is slow enough to give you time to find the next chord.

2. Play the left hand in the A section as broken chords, exactly the way the left hand is written. Learn this in the correct tempo of the piece and with the correct articulation. Be certain that the left hand is light. The first beat is stressed slightly more than the other beats.

3. Practice the right hand alone in the A section concentrating on and listening for
  • correct fingering
  • peaks of phrases
  • buoyant and light articulation

4. Learn the A section hands together, slowly at first, and gradually working the tempo up to a faster one. Work hard on making the left hand lighter and softer than the right hand melody. We have already discussed these ways to practice balance:

- practicing melody *f* and the accompaniment *pp* with a big difference in sound between the hands
- practicing the melody the way it is written and playing the accompaniment on the surface of the keys (no sound)
- playing the first note of each measure with the melody *f* and the accompaniment note *pp*
- playing a single note in both hands together at the base of the music rack to achieve weight in the right hand for the melody and to keep the left hand note light (brush the wood of the piano)

Still another way to practice balance and voicing is to play a passage like this only two or three times a day on the top of a table, feeling the melody louder and feeling the accompaniment softer.

5. Learn the third line as you did in step 1 above. Counting 1 & 2 & for each measure, play blocked octaves on beats 1 and 2 and use the &'s to find the next octave. Remember to take a tempo that is not too fast so that you can find the next octave without hesitating.

6. Now follow steps 2, 3, and 4 above for the third line.

7. Learn the last line hands separately first, and then hands together. Listen as you did above. Be sure that the surprising accents are surprises—small accents, not heavy.

8. Learn both parts of the B section. Work slowly at first. You will want to concentrate on achieving and hearing:

- buoyant staccatos
- light left hand accompaniment
- the focal point of each phrase
- surprises
- accurate rhythm that shows one beat, not four in a measure

9. Combine the A and B sections of this piece, and then practice it A B A. Listen carefully for the same things as in No. 8 above.

Finishing for performance

Ask yourself:

Do you hear the affect that you decided on?
Do you hear big dynamic differences between the sections?
Do you hear the surprises?
Are the surprises just that, and not heavy accents or harsh sounds?
Is the left hand light and buoyant?
Do you hear one or two pulses per measure, never four?
Does your performance flow so that it could be a dance?

Now focus your practice so that you are able to answer "yes" to all of the questions above! Your ear will tell you.

To the Teacher

Affect: sprightly, bouncing
Form: ABA; popular dance in 2/4
Number of ideas: first, third, and fourth lines use different melodic material and create different textures
Balance: right hand melody above left hand chords; chords are thick and will need careful work in keeping them soft
Phrase definition: extremely regular
Symmetry: repetition of phrase; balanced phrase lengths

This piece helps a student develop:

- balance of melody and thick, broken-chord accompaniment
- projection of humor in performance
- buoyancy of thick texture

Notes:

The texture is the thickest of any piece the student may have worked on to this point.

A feeling of one pulse (or possibly two pulses) per measure is fundamental to portraying the dance character of this piece.

To help the student hear the question and answer phrases, the teacher can play measures 1 and 2 of each line while the student answers, playing measures 3 and 4 of the line.

Romantic Period

Priming for the Pinnacle

The piano music of the Romantic era takes us in several directions. On the one hand, there is the music that is lyrical and melodic. It is often slow and singing. Generally this music features a beautiful cantabile melody over a quieter, atmospheric accompaniment. Listen to some of the Chopin *Nocturnes* to get an idea of this feeling.

Then, there are a large number of pieces composed in the Romantic period which are character pieces. Character pieces often are in A B A form. They are relatively short pieces, but seem to have a definable mood or character to them. Sometimes they are "programmatic." That is, the title or some other indication tells us why they might have been written. Many of the lyrical pieces fall into the category of character pieces also.

Another kind of piece found often in Romantic period piano music is the etude. Etudes frequently concentrate on one figure throughout the piece. Some etudes are fast and brilliant. In playing these the performer gains both musical and technical skill. He sharpens his ear for hearing and playing passages cleanly. The Romantic period features many other pieces which are not etudes and which concentrate on one figure all the way through. Etudes and additional pieces which point in this direction in the Romantic period literature in this section will be labeled here as "perpetual-motion pieces."

Naturally some pieces may fall into two of these categories. The categories are listed so that the performer will be aware of trends in Romantic period literature. It is essential that a pianist become well-rounded and capable of playing music which follows all of the various directions that the Romantic period composers took.

Programmatic Descriptions

Often music in the Romantic period has a story, a picture, or a thought that the composer intentionally associated with the piece. In many instances this is reflected in the title. This thought or story is not a musical one, but rather one that relates to events outside of music. Pieces with descriptive titles or with written notes from the composer concerning the mood or the story he had in mind when composing it are called "programmatic" pieces. Whereas in the Baroque, it was up to the performer to discern what "affect" the composer had in mind, in the Romantic period the composer frequently tells us the program for the piece. Most of the Romantic pieces in this volume are programmatic. The titles are indications of the mood and character that the composer had in mind. Sometimes this mood applies to the entire piece. On other occasions the title or program will tell or follow a story that happens in the music.

Texture in Romantic Period Music

The piano was still a relatively new instrument in 1825, but became very popular during the Romantic period. Composers began to write in a way that would take advantage of this instrument that could sound much louder than the harpsichord and clavichord. The music that they began to write for the piano used thicker chords and sometimes featured two melodies and accompaniment at once. These thicker textures (like thick material or cloth) required the pianist to specifically practice making the melody heard above the texture. The single note of the melody often should be played in a way that it will be heard above the many notes of the accompaniment chords below. Many artists do the same thing in painting. In painting a picture, they will make one color brighter for contrast or to bring out that color. Voicing the texture in music becomes an important consideration in playing pieces from the Romantic period. While balance between the hands, usually melody and accompaniment, had been extremely important in playing Classic period music, the emphasis now is on even more sound and bigger and fuller chords. Consequently, the pianist is called on to voice the melody over the whole texture, or to voice inner melodies within the texture.

Rubato in Romantic Period Music

A kind of give and take in the rhythm becomes more prevalent in Romantic period music. The composer often writes ritards in the music. If the give and take is subtle, it is called rubato. Technically, rubato indicates a kind of flexibility in the rhythm, in which one hand stays steady and the other fluctuates slightly. Usually it is the melody hand that fluctuates while the accompaniment hand remains steady. While it seems impossible at first, performers who do this are able to achieve rubato with extreme subtlety and finesse.

Many pianists add too much rubato to the music. A good key to remember in performing a ritard is to count while slowing down. The counting will slow gradually, thus not allowing you to suddenly slow down. Performers who speed up and slow down excessively can damage the performance of Romantic period music. Always count out ritards and let them happen easily and naturally.

Expression and Emotion

Expression in the Romantic period is not as restrained as it was in the Classic period. Romantic period expression in music is often emotional. Since the Romantic period in time was volatile, the music of this period is meant to be highly expressive and emotional. Finding the meaning behind the music (often the program is a guide) is essential in playing this music. Strong contrast of moods often occurs in the bigger works. Look for this strong contrast of emotion and for powerful feelings to portray in the music.

Romantic Literature

Listed for each piece are performance considerations which are emphasized in the selection

Bagatelle, Op. 68, No. 5 .... Schumann
- legato and phrasing
- rounding of phrases
- balance of melody and accompaniment

Soldier's March, Op. 68, No. 2 .... Schumann
- balance of melody and chords
- feeling for chord playing

Scherzo, Op. 140, No. 17 .... Gurlitt
- balance of melody and chords
- feeling for chord playing
- movement about the keyboard

The Music Box, Op. 140, No. 8 .... Gurlitt
- feeling for chord playing
- attention to fingering changes
- motor skills between the hands

Morning Song, Op. 140, No. 2 .... Gurlitt
- feeling for chord playing
- fingering changes between chords
- voicing melody over thick texture

March, Op. 140, No. 1 .... Gurlitt
- feeling for chord playing
- rhythmic coordination in left hand
- detail in articulation

The Wild Rider, Op. 68, No. 8 .... Schumann
- feeling for rapid chord passages
- motor coordination between hands
- balance of melody and thick accompaniment
- projection of left hand melody

The Little Beggar, Op. 123, No. 2 .... Gretchaninoff
- chord playing
- legato and phrasing
- coordination of syncopated rhythms
- balance of melody and chordal accompaniment

Bagatelle, Op. 68, No. 5   **Schumann**

See *Masterwork Classics 3*, page 25.

Getting ready to play

*(Write the answers in this book and on the music in **Masterwork Classics**.)*

A "bagatelle" is a short piece that is not not meant to be big and profound like a sonata. Schumann said to play it "not fast." Sight-read the melody of this piece to see if the one mood continues through the entire piece. What is that mood? _____

What does the form appear to be? _____

Which hand plays the melody? _____ In the left hand, circle the notes on the strong beats. Now play the circled notes. They move in the same direction as the melody (parallel) all the way through. They accompany the melody.

Which hand should be played softer than the other? _____ Why? _____ Which finger might tend to sound too loud in the left hand unless you are careful to play it lightly? (*Hint:* It is your strongest finger!) _____

Place brackets around the phrases in this piece. Place an arrow at the goal of each phrase. This is the same as the magnet note, the note to which all of the notes before it crescendo. You will want to make the music pull to the magnet note as you shape the phrase.

Practicing for performance

(Answer the questions in your mind and through the way you practice.)

Practice step by step. Be sure that you do not move ahead until you have met all of the thought and sound goals for the previous step that you have worked on. These goals come from what you have learned about earlier pieces as well as what is written in the step. Your ear will tell you when you have learned a step well enough to move ahead! When you practice the next day, you will want to go back several steps to practice and review what you have learned in earlier practice.

1. Learn the right hand alone with the music pulling toward the magnet note. Listen carefully for a smooth legato and for no bumps in your tone. Play so that the listener will know which note is the magnet note.

2. Learn the left hand alone, being especially careful to play the thumb notes softly and to pull to the focal point of the phrase.

3. Learn both hands together in the A section. Practice very slowly at first. Listen for
- smooth legato
- the focal point of the phrase
- a quiet left hand thumb
- the left hand softer than the right hand

Gradually work the tempo up to a slightly faster one. This piece is smooth and singing—it is lyrical. Make it sound like water flowing.

4. Learn both hands together for the B section. Follow the same listening guide that you did in No. 3.

5. Combine both sections of this piece. Listen carefully to be sure that you continue to keep a legato sound. If you reach a spot where you do not play well when taking a faster tempo, slow down the tempo and work out the detail here.

Finishing for performance

(Answer the questions in your mind.) Ask yourself:

Do you hear peaks of all phrases?

Is the legato smooth and very connected?

Do you hear the melody sing out over the accompaniment?

Can someone describe your playing as "lyrical," that is, smooth and connected?

Do you hear bumps in the phrases?

Practice now with your goal to be able to answer "yes" to all of these questions.

To the Teacher

Focus of the piece: to develop lyricism

Affect/program: simple "bagatelle," short piece, in which melody might flow like water

Balance/voicing: right hand above left hand accompaniment; melody is doubled at the tenth in the left hand; light left hand thumb will need practice

Fingering: relatively stationary positions; some left hand extensions to an octave

This piece helps a student develop:
- legato
- sense of phrasing
- balance of melody and accompaniment

Notes:
The student should be especially careful not to begin phrases with an accent. Since the thumb of the right hand presents the first note of many of the phrases, students should be encouraged to "sneak" into phrase beginnings.

Soldier's March, Op. 68, No. 2   **Schumann**

See *Masterwork Classics 3*, page 26.

Getting ready to play

The title of this piece, "Soldier's March," is programmatic in that it tells us ahead of time what the piece may be about. You will notice that the piece seems to be light rather than serious. It might be a march for young people in a make-believe parade or who are "playing soldier." Would you think that this piece would be played in a heavy or light way? _____

Sight-read the right hand melody. Do you see a place where the music contrasts so strongly that the mood would change? _____

Place brackets around the phrases in this piece. Then place an arrow at the focal point of each phrase. Are the phrases predictable in length? _____

Measures 1-8 form a section. Label it A. Notice that measures 9-16 are different entirely. Label this part B. The final section, measures 17-24, is similar to the A section but the last phrase is different. Label it A' since it is almost like the original A section. The form of this is A B A'.

In measures 1-2, which note is the same in every right-hand chord? _____

Write the rhythmic motive (distinct rhythmic pattern) that begins each phrase. _____

Practicing for performance

Practice step by step. Be sure that you do not move ahead until you have met all of the thought and sound goals for the previous step that you have worked on. These goals come from what you have learned about earlier pieces as well as what is written in the step. Your ear will tell you when you have learned a step well enough to move ahead! When you practice the next day, you will want to go back several steps to practice and review what you have learned in earlier practice.

1. In learning any piece, it is always better to spend more time practicing hands together than hands separately. Hands separate practice is best when first learning a section. It helps you see patterns and notice the correct fingering. You may not need to practice this piece hands separately very much at all.

2. In measures 1-4 play simultaneously the top note of the right hand and the bottom note of the left hand. Do they move in the same direction or opposite directions?

3. Now complete the learning of measures 1-4 by playing hands together. Notice the correct fingering and listen to pull the phrase to the magnet note.

4. Follow the same procedure as in Nos. 2 and 3 for measures 5-8.

5. Learn measures 9-16 as in Nos. 2 and 3.

6. Learn measures 17-24 in the same way as in Nos. 2 and 3.

7. Combine the phrases in the different sections. Learn the A section, listening for light accompaniment in the left hand, one pulse every two measures, and for the goals of phrases.

8. Learn the B section as you did the A section in No. 8, listening for the same goals.

9. Last, learn the final A' section as you did in No. 8.

10. Combine all sections of this piece. Keep the rhythm flowing and remember the "program" for this piece, practicing to be sure that your performance matches that story.

Finishing for performance

Ask yourself:

Do you hear one pulse for every two measures?
Do you hear goals of phrases?
Does your performance reflect the title of the piece?
Do you hear a light left hand?
Do you hear the phrases flow?

Practice now with your ear as your teacher so that you can answer "yes" to all of these questions.

To the Teacher

Focus of the piece: perpetual motion—one idea throughout

Affect/program: light march for children "playing soldier"

Form: A B A'

Balance/voicing: right hand double-note chords over left hand; top of right hand notes should project

Fingering: shifts needed for the chord changes throughout

Coordination: note-against-note style; fingering shifts are the main coordination concern

Contrast: same rhythmic movement and consistent texture throughout

This piece helps a student develop:
  • keyboard feeling for chordal playing
  • balance of right hand melody at the top of two-note chords

Notes:
  Correct fingering should be emphasized when learning chords in this piece.

Scherzo, Op. 140, No. 17

Gurlitt

See *Masterwork Classics 3*, page 27.

Getting ready to play

A "scherzo" is a light, humorous piece. Sometimes it is like a joke expressed in music. Look for any occasions of "jokes" in this piece. You will notice the marking *sf* on the third beats of many measures. These sudden stresses on a beat that is not normally accented are little jokes. The composer has put them there as sudden surprises for the listener. When you play the stresses, make them sound like surprises. Be careful that they are not too loud and or heavy. At the end in measures 20-25, the composer puts the accents on the "right" beat in the measure, the first beat!

Sight-read the right hand melody in this piece to listen for any changes of mood or contrast. What affect or character indication would you give to this piece to describe it? _____

Bracket phrases in this piece. How many measures in length do you expect a phrase to be? _____ Does this piece follow your expectation? _____

How many phrases are in this piece? _____ Does that uneven number surprise you? _____ That shows one way in which music in the Romantic period is not as symmetrical or balanced as that in the Classic period.

Can you divide this piece into sections—or is it composed all the way through (one large section)? _____

Each phrase (except the last one) begins with an upbeat that has a distinctive rhythm. Write that rhythm here. _____

Do you think that repeating a short and simple idea three times in a row, such as happens in the first phrase, is another sign of the composer's joking mood? _____

Practicing for performance

Practice step by step. Be sure that you do not move ahead until you have met all of the thought and sound goals for the previous step that you have worked on. These goals come from what you have learned about earlier pieces as well as what is written in the step. Your ear will tell you when you have learned a step well enough to move ahead! When you practice the next day, you will want to go back several steps to practice and review what you have learned in earlier practice.

1. You will want to learn this piece in phrases and by common patterns that occur in several phrases. Learn the left hand chords alone in measures 1-4. Then learn them in measures 5-8 and measures 17-20.

2. Learn the right hand alone for the same measures as you did in No. 1.

3. Combine both hands for measures 1-4, measures 5-8, and measures 17-20. Listen carefully to be sure that the left hand is not louder than the right hand melody.

4. The third phrase, measures 9-12 (with upbeats), has a figure that is repeated three times. Notice that it is played once high on the piano, then down an octave, and then again up in its original location. After you learn this in the three places without stopping the rhythm, add the last two chords of this phrase. Keeping the rhythm consistent through this phrase is very important.

5. Learn phrase seven, measures 25-28 (the final chords in the piece), first hands separately and then together. As is the case with any phrase, much more of your practice should occur playing the hands together rather than hands separately.

6. Now begin to combine your phrases in this piece. Work so that you can play the first two phrases, measures 1-8, with no stumbles and with consistent rhythm. Listen for the dynamic levels and for appropriate *sf*'s—not too loud. Then add the third phrase to this.

7. Since the fourth phrase, measures 13-16, is the same as the first, work to combine the fourth and fifth phrases in this piece. When learned well, continue by adding the sixth phrase. Work so that you can play phrases four, five, and six with correct fingering, appropriate dynamics and *sf*'s, and no stumbles. Be sure your playing sounds like the piece is a "scherzo." Finally add the last phrase to phrases four through six. Work for the same goals.

8. Combine both groups of phrases in this piece. Work for the same goals as in No. 7 above. Be sure that your playing is light and the rhythm buoyant. Remind yourself of what a "scherzo" should sound like.

Finishing for performance

Ask yourself:

Do you hear the right hand melody above the left hand chords?

Do you hear light buoyant left hand chords?

Do you hear *sf*'s that sound like small accents at unexpected times?

Do you hear one pulse per measure?

Does your piece sound like a "scherzo?"

Practice now with your ear as your teacher so that you can answer "yes" to all of these questions.

To the Teacher

Focus of the piece: character piece developing chordal playing

Affect/program: joke in music

Form: through-composed

Balance/voicing: melody above four-note chords on strong beats

Fingering: hand position moves about the keyboard

Coordination: moving of both hands about the keyboard

This piece helps a student develop:

• balance of single-note right hand melody above chordal left hand accompaniment

• a feeling of buoyancy and lightness in a chordal selection

Notes:

"Scherzo" needs a light, airy feeling. Left-hand chords may tend to make the texture sound thick and heavy unless the teacher stresses lightness and the feeling of one pulse per measure.

The Music Box, Op. 140, No. 8

Gurlitt

See *Masterwork Classics 3*, page 28.

See *Masterwork Classics 3*, page 29.

Getting ready to play

What do you expect a music box to sound like? _____
The title "The Music Box" is an example of a "programmatic" romantic title. That means that the title tells you a story about the piece or gives a meaning that the composer had in mind. Which clef do both hands play in? _____ How does that register help portray the sound of a music box? _____

Counting carefully, tap out the rhythm for the right hand in the first line. Next tap the right hand rhythm beginning with measure 17. Next, at measure 17, tap the right hand rhythm on your leg with the right hand and the left hand rhythm with the left hand. Finally, tap the rhythm of right hand and left hand at measure 25.

Sight-read the right hand melody all the way through. Place brackets around the phrases. Then place an arrow at the peak of each phrase.

What is the difference between measures 1-8 and measures 9-16? _____ The section that begins in measure 9 is transposed. It is the same as the section that began in measure 1 but it is transposed to the key of G.

Compare the way the notes look on the page in measure 17 with measure 1. The "texture" of both of these sections is different. That gives you one clue that this is a new section at measure 17. At measure 25 the melody of the A section returns. Do you notice that the accompaniment in the left hand still looks like it did for the previous section? _____ In a way, the first and the third sections are combined here. This piece is in four sections. The third is the most different from the others.

Look at the fingering in the third section. Notice that the first two notes of the right hand in each measure are the same. Sometimes the fingering will change even though the notes are the same. Circle the measures in which the fingering on the second note is different from the first. In which measures does this happen? _____

List the dynamic plan for this piece by section below.

Section one	measures 1-8	_____
Section two	measures 9-16	_____
Section three	measures 17-24	_____
Section four	measures 25-33	_____

Place brackets around the phrases. (Be careful as you read the right hand melody to hear that your rhythm is correct. It is always difficult to relearn something that was incorrect at first.) Then place arrows at the focal points of the phrases.

Practicing for performance

Practice step by step. Be sure that you do not move ahead until you have met all of the thought and sound goals for the previous step that you have worked on. These goals come from what you have learned about earlier pieces as well as what is written in the step. Your ear will tell you when you have learned a step well enough to move ahead! When you practice the next day, you will want to go back several steps to practice and review what you have learned in earlier practice.

1. Tap the rhythm for the right hand in the A section counting aloud

2. Play only the first note of the right hand in each measure with the correct finger. Be sure that you are playing "in time." Do this for measures 1-8. When you can do this well, follow this step for measures 9-16.

3. Now play the right hand alone for measures 1-8 with correct fingering and rhythm. Listen to be sure the phrases are smooth and that you hear the focal points of each phrase. Follow by doing the same thing in measures 9-16.

4. Play the left hand alone in measures 1-8. Which note is the same all the way through? Do your eyes look at the top or at the the bottom note for the left hand? Follow the same idea in measures 9-16.

5. Learn measures 1-8 hands together and measures 9-16 hands together. Work to make the performance smooth and connected. Listen to hear goals of phrases. Be sure there are no punched notes in your melody. The goal of the phrase should be the loudest note, but the goal should never be accented.

6. Tap the rhythm again in both hands for measures 17-24. Be sure the the flow of the rhythm is smooth and continuous.

7. Play the right hand alone in measures 17-20, paying special attention to correct fingering. Learn this so that you play the correct fingering each time and so that the phrase pulls to the magnet note.

8. As you look at the left hand in measures 17-20, notice the left hand note that is the same in each measure. Discover the left hand pattern for the first note in each measure and then play the left hand alone.

9. As you now combine both right hand and left hand in measures 17-20, listen to be sure that your notes are very smooth and connected between hands. Listen for the magnet note in the phrase. Be sure that every fingering is absolutely correct. Measures 21-24 are the same as measures 17-20. Combine both phrases in the B section.

10. In section four, the right hand is the same as in the first section. The left hand contains the same notes as it did in section one, but it uses the rhythm of section three. Practice this part hands together, listening for peaks of phrases and checking on fingering.

11. Practice the following phrases one after another so that you can hear the different dynamic levels of each section:

Section one	measures 1-4	play *p*
Section two	measures 9-12	play *mf*
Section three	measures 17-20	play *p*
Section four	measures 25-28	play *pp*

Let your ear hear the difference.

12. Combine sections one, two, and three of this piece.

13. Combine sections three and four of this piece.

14. Now work on the entire piece as a whole. Keep listening for the same goals as those you aimed for earlier. Since notes die away quickly on the piano, listen to be sure that you sneak into notes which come after rests or after the dotted quarters.

Finishing for performance

Ask yourself:

Do you hear smoothly shaped phrases?

Do you hear the magnet note of each phrase?

Do you hear smooth sounds without punched or accented notes?

Do you hear the right hand sing out above the left hand accompaniment?

Do you hear different dynamic levels for each section?

Practice now with your ear as your teacher so that you can answer "yes" to all of these questions.

To the Teacher

Focus of the piece: changing figuration and texture in a character piece

Affect/program: four different sections all sounding like a music box at different pitch and dynamic levels and with varied textures

Form: four eight-measure sections

Balance/voicing: melody above blocked-chord and later broken-chord accompaniment

Fingering: special attention should be given to the first right hand finger number of each measure; it sets the hand for the measure

Coordination: measures 17-33 require intricate timing between the hands

Contrast: four sections are set apart by dynamic changes and texture changes

This piece helps a student develop:

• the timing of fine rhythmic coordination between hands

• attention to fingering changes

Notes:

Although "The Music Box" was written in 3/8, the eventual sound will be as if it were written "in 2." Teachers may want to have the student count 1-2 in each measure despite the 3/8 indication. The performance of this piece "in 3" at the appropriate tempo does not feel right. The music <u>sounds</u> and <u>looks</u> on the page as if it is "in 2" even though it is written in triple meter.

The timing of the left hand rhythmic entries in the third section is difficult and will need slow practice for coordination. The tempo of the piece should be set with the coordination of both hands in the third and the fourth sections in mind.

Morning Song, Op. 140, No. 2   **Gurlitt**

See *Masterwork Classics 3*, page 30.

See *Masterwork Classics 3*, page 31.

Getting ready to play

What mood or character would you expect in a piece that is titled "Morning Song?" _____

How long do you expect the phrases to be? _____
Sight-read the right hand melody in this piece and place brackets around the phrases. Then place an arrow over the point of greatest tension in each phrase.

How long is the first section of this piece? _____ List the measures later in the piece where this section repeats. _____ _____ Are the repetitions exactly the same? _____ The middle section, measures 9-16, should be labeled B. Does the B section return? _____ Are both appearances of B the same? _____ The form of this piece is A B A B A.

Look more closely at the B section. What is the only difference between the two phrases, measures 9-12 and measures 13-16, in the B section? _____ Look more closely at the A section. What is the only difference between the two phrases, measures 1-4 and measures 5-8, in the A section? _____ How many <u>different</u> measures are there in this piece? _____

Practicing for performance

Practice step by step. Be sure that you do not move ahead until you have met all of the thought and sound goals for the previous step that you have worked on. These goals come from what you have learned about earlier pieces as well as what is written in the step. Your ear will tell you when you have learned a step well enough to move ahead! When you practice the next day, you will want to go back several steps to practice and review what you have learned in earlier practice.

1. When learning chords, let your eyes focus on the notes that change between the chords. You do not need to keep concentrating on the notes that stay the same. In measures 1-2 for each hand, place one long circle around the notes that change between the chords. Now practice these two measures hands together. In measures 3 and 4, a note in the left hand stays the same. Circle the changing notes here too. Now learn these two measures. Continue by learning measures 7-8.

2. Learn measures 1-4 as a phrase, listening for the goal of the phrase and a smooth sound. Practice the same way in measures 5-8.

3. Learn the right hand in measures 9-10 by playing the top and bottom notes in that hand only (sixths). When you can do this comfortably, play the right hand alone with all of the inner notes. Learn the left hand alone in those same two measures. When a melody moves in one direction and the other part moves in another direction as happens here, the lines are in contrary motion. Your hands move toward each other here, in contrary motion. Practice these two measures hands together.

4. Learn measures 11-12 hands together. Then practice measures 15-16 hands together.

5. Combine all of the parts of the B section. Listen carefully for a smooth line and work for correct fingerings.

6. Now combine the A and B sections. At first practice only the first A and first B sections. Since the rest of the piece repeats, you do not need to continue yet. Listen carefully for any places that might sound uneven or not smooth.

7. Work on the piece as a whole now. Listen carefully for dynamic differences and for smooth sounds. Try to make your performance sound like a "morning song."

Finishing for performance

Ask yourself:

Do you hear the goal of each phrase?
Do you hear smooth sounds?
Does the rhythm flow smoothly and evenly?
Do you hear the phrases taper gently at the ends?
Do you hear one pulse per measure?

Practice so that you can answer "yes" to each of these questions.

To the Teacher

Focus of piece: to develop lyricism

Affect/program: gentle morning song, perhaps with the sun appearing over the horizon

Form: A B A B A

Balance/voicing: melody above thick chordal texture

Fingering: fingering of parallel chords needs attention

Coordination: chord changes need attention

Contrast: derived totally from a change from parallel to contrary voice movement and a change of the rhythmic phrasing

This piece helps a student develop:
- playing of chordal pieces
- fingering of parallel triads
- voicing melody over thick texture

March, Op. 140, No. 1   Gurlitt

See *Masterwork Classics 3*, page 32.

See *Masterwork Classics 3*, page 33.

Getting ready to play

The title "March" might refer to a group of people pretending that they they are marching in a parade.

Write the rhythm of the right hand in measures 1-2. _____
_____ Circle this rhythm throughout the piece in *Masterwork Classics* whenever you find it in either hand. It forms a rhythmic motive (short rhythmic idea) that unifies "March."

To determine the form of this piece, look to see if you can define sections. In what measures do you see the theme in measures 1-2 repeated? _____ Check to see how much of the section beginning in measure 1 is repeated each of those times. New material begins in measure 17. Measures 1-8 and measures 9-16 are the same except for the last two measures of each section. Measures 25-32 are the same as measures 9-16. The form of this piece is A A' B A'.

Place brackets around the phrases here. How long do you expect them to be? _____ Place an arrow at the focal point of each phrase.

Write the articulation for the right hand in measure 2. _____ List the measures in this piece that have that same articulation. _____ Remember that the last note of a two-note slur is played staccato here.

Practicing for performance

Practice step by step. Be sure that you do not move ahead until you have met all of the thought and sound goals for the previous step that you have worked on. These goals come from what you have learned about earlier pieces as well as what is written in the step. Your ear will tell you when you have learned a step well enough to move ahead! When you practice the next day, you will want to go back several steps to practice and review what you have learned in earlier practice.

1. Throughout the entire piece play only the hand and measures that have the rhythmic motive you wrote above. Be sure that you use the exact articulation.

2. Practice the right hand in measures 6 and 7 and the left hand in measure 8.

3. Learn, within a continuous tempo, the right hand in measures 1-2, left hand in measures 3-4, and right hand for measures 5-8. Be sure the fingering is played exactly as the music says. Work slowly at first to get it exactly right. Once you can do this, it will be especially easy to put the other part with it.

4. Practice measures 1-8 hands together listening for and concentrating on
   - correct fingering
   - exact articulation
   - focal points of phrases
   - exact rhythm (especially measures 7 and 8)

5. Practice measures 14-16. This is the part of the A' section that is different from the A section. After practicing the A' section as a whole, then combine A and A'.

6. Look at the B section and notice the repetition. Measures 19-20 are exactly like measures 17-18 except for one note. Learn these four measures. What note in measures 21-24 makes the change to lead back to the A section? Practice these measures hands together.

7. Combine both phrases in the B section. Be very careful to have the articulation just right.

8. Combine the B section and final A' section. Listen to make the rhythm very solid and stable like a march. Listen also for the sound goals mentioned in the steps above.

9. Combine all of the sections of the piece. Make your performance sound like a march that children might move to. Make it sound like the programmatic title.

Finishing for performance

Ask yourself:

Do you hear a solid and steady rhythm?

Do you hear a firm sound that is not too loud or too heavy?

Do you hear one pulse per measure?

Do you hear the exact articulation written in the music?

Does your performance sound like a piece that young people could march to?

Practice now with the goal of making your answer be "yes" to all of these questions.

To the Teacher

Focus of the piece: character piece

Affect/program: young people's march, perhaps for a parade

Form: A A' B A'

Balance/voicing: double-note melody needing the top brought out over double-note and single-note accompaniment

Fingering: needs care with crossings but not particularly tricky

Coordination: detailed articulation; rhythmic left hand movement under sustained right hand

Contrast: no change in character in the B section

This piece helps a student develop:

• intricate rhythmic coordination between hands

  • detailed articulation

  • playing of chordal passages

Notes:

The coordination of the left hand rhythmic figures in measures 3-4 and similar measures against an independent right hand will need special attention.

The feeling of one pulse per measure is essential to prevent a heavy, stodgy sound.

The Wild Rider, Op.68, No. 8

Schumann

See *Masterwork Classics 3*, page 34.

See *Masterwork Classics 3*, page 35.

Getting ready to play

The programmatic title, "The Wild Rider," might indicate to us that this piece is about a horseman who gallops along in the countryside. Notice the many interval skips in the melody which could portray the horse galloping. Sight-read the melody in the right hand in measures 1-8, in the left hand in measures 9-16, and in the right hand again in measures 17-24. Do you hear a large contrast that would call for a different mood in the middle section? _____ Which section is in major and which is in minor? _____

How long might you expect the phrases to be? _____ Place brackets around all of the phrases. Then place an arrow at the peaks of phrases. Where do the *sf*'s occur in each phrase? _____ Is this at the same place in each phrase? _____ Did the peak of the phrase coincide with the *sf* in any of the phrases? _____

All of the melody notes are played staccato except those where the slur covers two notes. Does the *sf* occur at the same time? _____ Will the second note under the two-note slur be played staccato? _____

In determining the form for this piece, look first for any repeat signs or double-bars. The repeat sign in measure 8 might indicate the end of a section. Also the double bar in measure 16 might do the same. At measure 16, you notice that the melody and accompaniment at measure 1 repeat. The entire first section, measures 1-8, repeats in measures 17-24. The melody from measures 1-8 appears in the left hand at measure 9-16 and in a new key. The accompaniment there is in the right hand. The form of this piece then is A B A.

Why do you think you will need to work especially hard to keep the accompaniment soft in this piece? _____

In the first two phrases of the piece, most of the measures repeat exactly. Which measures in each phrase are different? _____ The same thing happens in the B section. Which measures in each phrase here are different? _____

Practicing for performance

Practice step by step. Be sure that you do not move ahead until you have met all of the thought and sound goals for the previous step that you have worked on. These goals come from what you have learned about earlier pieces as well as what is written in the step. Your ear will tell you when you have learned a step well enough to move ahead! When you practice the next day, you will want to go back several steps to practice and review what you have learned in earlier practice.

1. Learn the right hand alone for the A section concentrating on and listening for
   - correct fingering
   - correct articulation
   - *sf*'s
   - one pulse in each measure

2. Learn the left hand chords for the A section, concentrating on and listening for the same goals as in No. 1.

3. As you begin to practice hands together for the A section, play very slowly so you can hear when the coordination is exactly right for both hands. Be careful also to play the articulation as it is written in the music.

4. Practice for balance between the hands in these ways:
- play right hand *f*, left hand *pp*
- play right hand sounding as usual, and the left hand on top of the keys with no sound
- play only the first and fourth beats of every measure hands together, very slowly, listening for balance
- play this on a table-top, feeling the correct balance
- feel the first beat of each measure on the fall-board of the piano (close the piano and use the cover) with the correct balance between hands; your left hand will be very light and should almost brush the wood

5. Follow the same process for Nos. 1-3 in learning the B section. You will learn the left hand melody first, as in No. 1, and follow the same steps.

6. Then work on balance between the hands in the B section practicing as you did in No. 4 above. Reverse the process, since you want the left hand melody to be louder than the right hand. You will need to practice this even longer than you did in No. 4. Be sure you hear the correct balance before you leave this step.

7. Combine all sections of this piece. Listen very carefully for balance between the hands as well as for the additional sound goals listed above.

8. Isolate all of the strong cadences. These are the chords that end the phrases. They occur in measures 4, 8, 12, 16, 20, and 24. Play these measures alone, listening for the endings of phrases so that the last chord is not accented.

9. Now return and practice the entire piece as a whole, listening to ends of phrases as well as other sound goals for "The Wild Rider."

Finishing for performance

Ask yourself:

Do you hear one pulse per measure?

Does your rhythm sound buoyant and lilting the way a horse might gallop?

Do you hear the melody project over the accompaniment?

Do you hear goals of phrases?

Do you hear phrases that end without accents?

Let your practice focus to make your answer become "yes" to all of these questions.

To the Teacher

Focus of piece: character piece

Affect/program: rider on horse galloping

Form: A B A

Balance/voicing: single-note melody and thick chordal accompaniment; melody in right hand, accompaniment in left hand in A section; melody in left hand, accompaniment in right hand in B section

Fingering: misfingerings may occur due to the consistent staccatos throughout the piece

Coordination: quick coordination of fast rhythmic figures in the accompaniment may be difficult at first

Contrast: B section contrasts in the use of major mode as opposed to minor in the A section and in the appearance of the same melody in a different voice from the A section

This piece helps a student develop:
- balance of melody and thick accompaniment
- projection of melody in left hand
- coordination of quick accompaniment rhythms with melody

Notes:

This piece should not be played too fast. The indication is "allegro," "happy." As the tempo increases, the coordination of the accompaniment figure in measure 2 and similar places will become more difficult. Arm tension from the too-fast repetitions could occur.

The Little Beggar, Op. 123, No. 2

Gretchaninoff

See *Masterwork Classics 3*, page 36.

Getting ready to play

This piece is marked "moderato." Sight-read the right hand and and define a mood for it. _____ Keep this mood in mind always when you practice it as THE word which characterizes this piece.

How many sections do you find? _____ Label them with A's and B's. (*Hint:* Do you find strong cadences in measures 4, 8, 12? _____ Play them.)

Circle the only chord in the two A sections that is different.

Which hand plays the melody? _____
      the accompaniment? _____

What is the first chord of the A sections? _____
               B section? _____

Carefully count and tap the rhythm of the first two measures of the right hand. Do it slowly, then a bit faster—several times in a row. Then tap the rhythm for the entire piece.

Play the right hand melody alone. Mark all phrases with brackets. Place an arrow above the magnet note in the melody (above the treble staff) in each phrase.

Practicing for performance

Practice step by step. Be sure that you do not move ahead until you have met all of the thought and sound goals for the previous step that you have worked on. These goals come from what you have learned about earlier pieces as well as what is written in the step. Your ear will tell you when you have learned a step well enough to move ahead! When you practice the next day, you will want to go back several steps to practice and review what you have learned in earlier practice.

1. Practice the right hand alone, shaping each phrase to pull to the magnet note and making certain that all fingering is correct.

2. Practice the left hand alone in measures 1 and 6 playing beats 1 and 2 together as a chord (this is called "blocking") and beats 3 and 4 as a chord. Play these chords back and forth continuously.

3. Work on the left hand the way it is written on the page.

4. Take all strong cadences—measures 4, 8, and 12 and their upbeats—and practice each slowly until you play it easily.

5. Learn measures 1 and 2, then measures 3 and 4. Then do the same with measures 5 and 6 and measures 7 and 8.

6. Put the entire B section together — slowly, then faster. Then do the same with the A sections.

7. Work on the musical elements in this piece
   • letting both hands shape toward the arrow in each phrase
   • playing the right hand melody *f*
                 left hand accompaniment *p*
so that the melody is balanced over the accompaniment.

8. Play all sections first slowly, then faster listening for
   • the character and mood
   • the phrase shapes and the magnet notes
   • a smooth legato with no punched notes

Finishing for performance

Ask yourself:

Do you hear a smooth legato with no punched notes?

Do the dynamics begin at different levels for the A, B, and A' sections?

Is the "poco rall." in measure 8 smooth?

Do you hear the phrases crescendo to the most important note?

Now practice so that you are able to answer "yes" to each of these questions. Change your way of playing when you need to so that the answer becomes "yes."

To the Teacher

Focus of the piece: character piece

Affect/program: insistent, in the mood of a "little beggar"

Balance/voicing: right hand melody must sound over left hand accompaniment chords

Form: A B A

Fingering: hands generally remain close to set positions

Coordination: rhythmic intricacies present the biggest problem; student must feel inner pulse

This piece helps a student develop:
   • coordination of syncopated rhythms
   • balance of single-note melody and chordal accompaniment

Notes:
   The short slurs in this piece should be interpreted as a sign to group notes together rather than as a sign to separate the sound. No break should be made between these groups. The sound of the piece becomes too "busy" when silences occur for all of these short slurs.

Contemporary Period

Priming for the Pinnacle

Is the pinnacle of performance for Contemporary music any different from that for the other periods? Not when referring to the conservative piano literature by such composers as Bartók, Kabalevsky, and Shostakovich. These composers followed in the footsteps of the tradition which preceded them. They built upon the sounds and sonorities developed in the Romantic period, and then expanded the harmonic language. It is primarily within the scope of playing twentieth-century avant-garde literature that the listening goals are expanded. Although avant-garde pieces are beyond the scope of this book, that music calls for an increased awareness of sound from the performer. The performer perhaps is listening differently to the sonority and the texture. To gain any increased aural awareness, a pianist cannot skip over the traditional contemporary literature which also stretches the ears.

The contemporary literature found in *Masterwork Classics* is limited to that written by early twentieth-century composers. This is the repertoire which is at the basis of modern music. It is literature which cannot be neglected because of its place in the development of sound and technique in twentieth-century music. These pieces often are rhythmic and need strong characterization of the mood or program. Students frequently play this music with ease and flair because of their strong identification with the rhythmic components and due to their identification with the more flamboyant side of performing. All of this is true also for some music of the various earlier periods. However, it is this combination of features found in many of the pieces by twentieth-century composers which makes them so attractive to many students.

Rhythmic Features

In all of the early twentieth-century literature in this volume, strong rhythm is a vital part of a successful performance. Rhythm is the heartbeat of music. It gives life and movement to music of our time. Phrase lengths may be asymmetrical, but the rhythm remains vital and strong. Often syncopations dot the score of this conservative music. These syncopations contribute as well to the vitality of the music.

Many piano composers have written toccatas for advanced performers. These pieces exploit both the brilliance of the instrument and a rhythmic pattern which is often unceasing. The rhythmic continuity gives the piece drive and energy.

Characterization and Expression

Music in this period needs the same strong characterization of mood or story that music in the Romantic period needed. Most of the works in this volume are given programmatic titles. The performer is told by the composer exactly what mood or image he had in mind when writing the piece. Twentieth-century music cannot be expressive without the characterization portrayed in the performance.

Harmonic Basis of Twentieth-Century Music

Music of our century has moved in so many directions that definition and tracing of the trends is impossible. The expanded harmonic language of much of today's music is reflected mildly in the pieces in this volume. These pieces retain key centers. The use of chromaticism and extended harmonies is present, but fits within the framework of traditional harmony.

Listed for each piece are performance considerations which are emphasized in the selection

Contemporary Period

"A Little Joke," Op. 39, No. 6 .... Kabalevsky
- detailed articulation
- discovery of patterns
- playing rapid staccato

"Funny Event," Op. 39, No. 7 .... Kabalevsky
- detailed articulation
- discovery of patterns
- playing rapid staccato
- inflection in single-note staccato passages

"Scherzo," Op. 39, No. 12 .... Kabalevsky
- detailed articulation
- discovery of patterns
- motor skills between hands
- playing rapid staccato
- quick rhythmic responses

"Jumping," Op. 39, No. 15 .... Kabalevsky
- detailed articulation
- discovery of patterns
- playing rapid staccato
- motor skills between hands
- quick rhythmic and dynamic responses

"A Fable," Op. 39, No. 14 .... Kabalevsky
- detailed articulation
- discovery of patterns
- playing rapid staccato
- quick rhythmic responses

"A Sad Story," Op. 39, No. 16 .... Kabalevsky
- playing of two-note slurs
- legato and phrasing
- discovery of patterns

"March," Op. 39, No. 10 .... Kabalevsky
- exact rhythmic response
- playing of four-note chords
- quick fingering shifts

"A Tale," Op. 98, No. 1 .... Gretchaninoff
- shifting hand position within and between phrases
- changing fingers on a single note

"A Tiresome Tale," Op. 98, No. 8 .... Gretchaninoff
- coordination of moving right hand melody over two-note slurs
- strong characterization of sequenced events

"A Lingering Song," Op. 98, No. 14 .... Gretchaninoff
- sustaining long melodic line
- balance melody and thick accompaniment

"The Bear" .... Rebikov
- voicing of melody above accompaniment
- coordination of independent rhythmic figures
- playing broken octaves

"March," Op. 98, No. 3 .... Gretchaninoff
- rounding short phrases

A Little Joke, Op. 39, No. 6

Kabelevsky

See *Masterwork Classics 3*, page 37.

To the Teacher

Affect/program: light mood and character of someone playing a joke

Balance: right hand melody is doubled at the sixth below in the left hand

Fingering: stationary hand positions, very little movement on the keyboard

Coordination: same figure in both hands

This piece helps a student develop:
- detail in articulation
- discovery of patterns

Notes:

Although no phrasing is indicated in the score, phrases should be carefully shaped. A dynamic plan and phrase goals should be heard.

The second note of the two-note slurs is played staccato.

Getting ready to play

*(Write the answers in this book and on the music in **Masterwork Classics**.)*

How do you expect a piece that is a little joke to sound? _____ Would you expect it to be heavy or light? _____ Does this piece appear to be primarily staccato or primarily legato? _____

Place brackets around the phrases. Then place an arrow over the note in each phrase that you think will be the most important. It is the focal point of that phrase—the point of greatest tension. You will let the phrase gradually crescendo to that note or chord.

When you play a note that has a staccato and a tenuto marking (⊤) over it as in measure 15, make that note slightly longer and stress it a bit.

Which hand plays the melody? _____ You will notice that the left hand doubles the right hand. That means that it sounds exactly like the right hand does, but on a different pitch.

Practicing for performance

(Answer the questions in your mind and through the way you practice.)

Practice step by step. Be sure that you do not move ahead until you have met all of the thought and sound goals for the previous step that you worked on. These goals come from what you have learned about earlier pieces as well as what you find written in the step. Your ear will tell you when you have learned a step well enough to move ahead! At the beginning of your practice the following day, you will want to go back several steps to practice and review what you have learned in earlier practice.

1. Find the starting hand position for this piece. Notice that your thumbs are on keys next to each other. As your hands move in this piece, your thumbs will remain in positions next to each other. Practice measures 1-2, being careful to play the staccatos in exactly the right places.

2. Continue by learning measures 1-4. Add measures 5-8. Which measure in this phrase is different from measures 1-4?

3. As you look at measures 9-14, you notice that each idea happens twice. In measures 9-10 the root of each hand in the pattern is D in left hand and B in right hand. In measures 11-12 both hands move down one key to C and A. In measures 13-14 both hands move down one key to B and G. Play all of the notes of each measure simultaneously as one chord so that you block the sound. Practice playing the three chords, hands together, to help learn the hand positions on the piano.

4. Practice measures 9-16 as written.

5. Now combine both sections of this piece. Be careful to listen for

- goals of phrases
- exact articulation
- light staccatos
- one pulse in every two measures

Finishing for performance

Ask yourself:

Did you hear a little joke in your performance?

Did you hear peaks of phrases?

Did you hear the phrases flow with one pulse in every two measures?

Did you hear nimble staccatos?

Practice letting your ear be your teacher as you work to make your answer be "yes" to all of these questions.

Funny Event, Op. 39, No. 7

Kabelevsky

Getting ready to play

Look at the music (do not play yet) and discover the funny event. Do you notice that each figure in the left hand is mimicked (repeated) by the right hand? _____ The right hand could be mocking the left hand. Or, you could say that the left hand and right hand are having a conversation.

Discover the form of this piece—that is, the way the composer has put it together. Do you see a section toward the middle or end that looks like the beginning section does? _____ Where in this piece does the rhythm change? _____ Does that give you a clue as to where the section might change? _____ Give the numbers for the measures that you think are in each section.

A _____
B _____
A _____

Is this piece primarily legato or staccato? _____ What measures have connected notes in them? _____

Place brackets around all of the phrases in this piece. Then place an arrow at the focal point of each phrase.

Write the dynamic marking at the beginning of each section.

A _____
B _____
A _____

Practice hint: Let your eyes focus on the first note of each measure. That way your eyes can see the entire measure as a group. Keep your eyes looking ahead of your hands as you play this piece. You will be able to play it more easily.

See *Masterwork Classics 3*, page 38.

Practicing for performance

Practice step by step. Be sure that you do not move ahead until you have met all of the thought and sound goals for the previous step that you worked on. These goals come from what you have learned about earlier pieces as well as what you find written in the step. Your ear will tell you when you have learned a step well enough to move ahead! At the beginning of your practice the following day, you will want to go back several steps to practice and review what you have learned in earlier practice.

1. Practice the A section first. Name aloud the first note of each measure. Can you memorize these notes even before you begin to play? Notice which finger begins the first note of each measure for the left hand. Then notice it for the right hand. Can you memorize these finger numbers also? Now practice the first phrase, being very careful that you play the articulation written exactly as the music indicates.

2. As you look at the B section, you will notice that these five-finger patterns descend (go down) in both hands, then ascend (go up) in both hands. Also, each five-finger pattern uses only white keys except for F-sharp. The dynamic markings indicate that when the patterns descend, the music should become softer. When the patterns ascend, the music should become louder. Practice both hands for this section listening for

- goals of phrases
- dynamic markings written in the music
- light staccatos

Did you notice that the first note of each pattern is one note higher than the note upon which the last pattern ended?

3. Combine all of the sections of this piece listening for

- goals of phrases
- dynamic differences between the sections
- light staccatos
- the conversation between both hands
- phrases that taper at the ends

Finishing for performance

Ask yourself:

Do you hear a conversation between the hands that could be a funny story if told in words?

Do you hear one pulse for every two measures?

Do you hear the dynamic plan that the composer wrote in the music?

Do you hear goals of phrases that you marked?

Do you hear light staccatos?

Do you hear phrases that taper at the ends?

Practice now with the goal of answering each question "yes." Your ear will tell you the correct answer.

To the Teacher

Affect/program: a humorous conversation where the right hand mimics what the left hand has "said" (played)

Form: A B A

Balance: entire piece is single-note melody alternating between hands

Fingering: no crossings; movement about the keyboard is limited

Coordination: playing of staccatos requires agile articulation

Contrast: dynamic contrasts for the sections

This piece helps a student develop:
- inflection in playing single-note melodies
- dynamic control of each finger
- playing of rapid staccato passages

Notes:
Accents at beginnings of measures should be light.

Scherzo, Op. 39, No. 12

Kabelevsky

Getting ready to play

A "scherzo" is a light, playful piece, often "joking" in nature. The Kabalevsky "Scherzo" is marked "vivo, giocoso," meaning "lively, humorous."

The skeleton of the melody occurs in the left hand fifth finger, the first note of each measure. Play that note through the entire piece and place brackets around the phrases in this piece. Then place an arrow at the focal note, the magnet note, of each phrase. How long are your phrases? _____

Write the rhythm that occurs in most of the measures in the first section. _____ What measures in the piece do not use that rhythm? _____ Tap the rhythm of the entire piece.

Which counts are played staccato in most measures? _____

Which note do you think will be the loudest in the entire piece? _____ Which note do you think will be the softest? _____

Practicing for performance

Practice step by step. Be sure that you do not move ahead until you have met all of the thought and sound goals for the previous step. These goals come from what you have learned about earlier pieces as well as what you find written in the step. Your ear will tell you when you have mastered a step well enough to move ahead! At the beginning of your practice the following day, you will want to go back several steps to practice and review what you have learned.

1. Cover all of the notes to be played by both hands in measure 1. Notice that your thumbs are next to each other on adjacent keys. They will remain next to each other for the entire piece. Block the chords for both hands in measure 1. Now practice the entire piece with blocked chords in both hands. All measures are based on chords except the last measure of the piece. Let your eyes focus on the first note of the left hand in each measure as you read the piece, since you already know that the hand position will be the same for each chord.

2. Practice this piece now by phrases. Learn the first phrase. When this is mastered, continue by practicing the second, third, and fourth phrases. The sound goals for each phrase are to listen for
- staccatos in exactly the right places
- goals of phrases
- light and precise staccatos
- strong rhythm

3. Combine the phrases of the piece. Learn measures 1-8 as a group and measures 9-16 as a group. When these groups meet the sound goals outlined above, practice the entire piece as a whole. Be sure you can hear the loudest note of the piece and the softest note of the piece.

Finishing for performance

Ask yourself:

Do you hear strong rhythm?
Do you hear the phrases flow?
Do you hear goals of the phrases?
Does your performance sound light and playful?
Do you follow the dynamic plan written in the music?

Let your ear be your teacher as you practice to make your answer become "yes" to each of these questions.

See *Masterwork Classics 3*, page 39.

To the Teacher

Affect/program: playful, joking

Form: four four-measure phrases

Balance: melody divided between both hands; first note in left hand in each measure is melody skeleton

Fingering: hands remain in five-finger positions and move the set position about the keyboard

Coordination: quick rhythmic response

This piece helps a student develop:
- quick rhythmic response
- precision in articulation
- discovery of patterns in music

Jumping, Op. 39, No. 15   Kabelevsky

See *Masterwork Classics 3*, page 40.

Getting ready to play

Would you expect a piece titled "Jumping" to feature staccato passages? _____ Would you expect to find intervals with skips (or jumps)? _____ Are both of these instances true for this piece? _____

Discover the form. Look for a section in the middle or near the end that seems to repeat the opening. In what measure does this repeat begin? _____ Which three measures at the end are different from the beginning section? _____ What dynamic markings do you see that might indicate the sections of this piece? _____

Mark the measures and dynamics in each section in this piece.

	measures	dynamic level
A	_____	_____
B	_____	_____
A'	_____	_____

The melody appears in different voices in the sections. The left hand plays the melody in the A sections. The right hand plays the melody in the B section.

Place brackets around the phrases in this piece. Then place an arrow at the focal point of each phrase. How long do you expect the phrases to be? _____

What similarities do the notes in the syncopated voice (voice with the eighth notes) have with the melody? _____

Practicing for performance

Practice step by step. Be sure that you do not move ahead until you have met all of the thought and sound goals for the previous step that you worked on. These goals come from what you have learned about earlier pieces as well as what you find written in the step. Your ear will tell you when you have learned a step well enough to move ahead! At the beginning of your practice the following day, you will want to go back several steps to practice and review what you have learned in earlier practice.

1. Practice the A section hands separately. Practice the melody (left hand) first. Then practice the syncopated accompaniment. Be very careful that you play the articulation exactly right. Listen for goals of phrases and for light staccatos.

2. Combine both hands in the A section. Be especially careful to play the articulation and rhythm just right. Listen to be sure the performance portrays a "jumping" mood.

3. Learn the B section in the same way that you practiced the A section. Here you will practice first the right hand melody and then the left hand accompaniment. Be especially careful to play the first finger number in the measure correctly, since that sets your hand position for the whole measure. If this finger is correct, all of the fingerings in the measure probably will be correct. It is especially important to play very lightly.

4. Practice the final A' section now. Begin with the last phrase, measures 21-24, since this contains the three measures that are different from the beginning A section. Work on them hands separately first. The fingering changes here—observe it carefully.

5. Combine the sections of the piece. First combine two sections. Work on A and B as a group. Also work on B and A' as a group. Finally work on the entire piece, following the same sound goals as outlined above. Be especially careful to practice moving smoothly from section to section. A special practice technique here would be to practice the last two measures of the A section and the first two measures of the B section with no stumbles. Then practice the last two measures of the B section and the first two measures of the A' section. Be careful to observe the dynamic changes!

Finishing for performance

Ask yourself:

Does your performance sound like you are jumping on tiptoes?
Do you hear light staccatos?
Do you hear goals of phrases?
Do you hear dynamic difference between the sections?
Are the dynamic changes between sections big ones?
Do you feel one pulse per measure in your playing?

Practice now with the goal of letting your answer be "yes" to all of these questions.

To the Teacher

Affect/program: jumping on tiptoes
Form: A B A'
Fingering: hand position for each measure is established by setting the correct finger for the first note of the measure
Coordination: quick syncopation, fine motor coordination
Contrast: dynamic change between sections

This piece helps a student develop:
- coordination of syncopated rhythms
- motor skills between the hands
- detail in articulation
- quick changes of dynamic level

Notes:
The fingering is more difficult in the B and A' sections than in the opening section. Placing the correct finger on the first note of the measure is essential.

A Fable, Op. 39, No. 14

Kabelevsky

See *Masterwork Classics 3*, page 41.

Getting ready to play

A "fable" is a fairy tale or a story. This fable is marked "allegro moderato," "happy and at a moderate tempo." Make up words for a story to fit the right hand melody.

Sight-read the right hand melody. How long do you expect the phrases to be? _____ How long are the phrases in this piece? _____ How many phrases do you find in this piece? _____ Place brackets around the phrases. Then place an arrow at the focal point of each phrase. This is the note to which all others in the phrase will pull.

Write the dynamic scheme and the measure numbers for the phrases here.

	measures	*dynamic level*
A	_____	_____
B	_____	_____
A	_____	_____

The difference between the notes in the A and B sections is slight. Notice which sharps are played in the A section and which sharps are not played in the B section. In this piece, the same phrase is played three times, first major, second minor, third major again. Notice how knowing this gives you even less material to learn in the piece.

Practicing for performance

Practice step by step. Be sure that you do not move ahead until you have met all of the thought and sound goals for the previous step that you worked on. These goals come from what you have learned about earlier pieces as well as what you find written in the step. Your ear will tell you when you have learned a step well enough to move ahead. At the beginning of your practice the following day, you will want to go back several steps to practice and review what you have learned in earlier practice.

1. Tap the rhythm for the right hand in the first phrase. Learn the right hand notes and rhythm for measures 3 and 4. Be very careful to play the two-note slur at the end of the measure. After this passage is learned very well, continue by learning the entire right hand for measures 1-4. Be certain that you play it well with correct fingering, and that you hear the goal of the phrase before continuing to the next step.

2. In measures 1-4, every other left hand note is the same. Circle the note that is different each time. Say aloud the names of the notes that are not repeated. Can you memorize this pattern? Practice the left hand alone listening carefully for
  • light staccatos
  • strong rhythm
  • light thumbs (the thumb is the strongest finger!)
  • the two-note slur at the end
  • the peak of the phrase
  • easy accents on the first note of each measure to set the pulse

3. Practice slowly and carefully combining both hands for the A section. It is best to practice slowly and to gradually increase the tempo. Listen for the same sound goals as in Nos. 1 and 2 above. Be certain that all of the articulation markings are correct. If the section is learned correctly here, it will be correct for the next two times that it is played in the piece.

4. Learn the B phrase, following the same steps as in Nos. 1-3 above.

5. Practice the final phrase of the piece to learn the change in the last measure.

6. Combine all of the phrases. Work and listen carefully to the dynamic contrast between sections and to goals of the phrases. Also listen to hear that the accents on the first beat of each measure are not heavy. Be sure to taper the end of each phrase.

Finishing for performance

Ask yourself:

Do you hear the peak of each phrase?

Does your performance sound like there are three phrases in this piece?

Do you hear the three dynamic contrasts between sections?

Do you hear buoyant and light staccatos that are very short?

Do you hear one pulse per measure?

Practice letting your ear be your guide as you listen to your playing, and practice so that your answer is "yes" to each of these questions.

To the Teacher

Affect/program: a happy story to be devised by the student; words added to the melody might help define phrasing

Form: three identical four-measure phrases played major-minor-major

Balance/voicing: melody over accompaniment

Fingering: minimal shifts

Coordination: playing of staccatos in rapid tempo and clarity of sixteenth passages

Contrast: major and minor sounds with contrasting dynamic levels

This piece helps a student develop:

• quick articulation of staccato passages

• coordination of rapid sixteenths above a moving accompaniment

Notes:

Exact control of the staccatos is important. This control aims toward independence of fingers as well as the development of tonal control in each finger.

A Sad Story, Op. 39, No. 16   Kabelevsky

See *Masterwork Classics 3*, page 41.

Getting ready to play

How would you expect this piece to sound based on the title given here? _____ "Andante" indicates that this should probably be played at a "walking" tempo. Can you think of a sad story or make up one that can help you with the mood of this piece? _____

Discover the form. Read through the right hand melody. Compare the notes of the melody in measures 1-7 with measures 17-23. One note is added to the melody in measures 18, 20, 22, and 23— but that is the only difference from the beginning. Is the left hand the same in measures 1-7 and measures 17-23? _____The middle section, measures 9-16 doubles the right hand melody in the left hand. This happened also in "A Little Joke." Circle the notes that the right hand thumb plays in each measure. Circle the notes that the left hand fifth finger plays in each measure. What is the pattern? _____The note that is not circled in measures 10, 12, and 14 is an E. Are there any added E's in the last phrase?
_____

Write the measures included in each section of this piece.

A _____
B _____
A' _____

Place brackets around the phrases in this piece. Then place an arrow at the focal point of each phrase. In looking for the focal point in the B section, listen to the bottom note (without the E's) to help guide your ear.

"A Sad Story" has many two-note slurs. These are two notes connected by a slur. Two-note slurs are very expressive markings and are played with special treatment. Stress the first note of a two-note slur and gently taper the second one. This kind of playing will make the piece sound like a "sad story." Circle all of the two-note slurs in this piece. Many pieces from the Classic period also feature two-note slurs.

Practicing for performance

Practice step by step. Be sure that you do not move ahead until you have met all of the thought and sound goals for the previous step that you worked on. These goals come from what you have learned about earlier pieces as well as what you find written in the step. Your ear will tell you when you have learned a step well enough to move ahead! At the beginning of your practice the following day, you will want to go back several steps to practice and review what you have learned in earlier practice.

1. Practice measures 1-8 hands separately. Concentrate on and listen for
- the goal of each phrase
- correct fingering
- tapered ends of phrases

2. Practice measures 1-8 hands together listening very carefully and concentrating on the goals above.

3. Learn the B section the same way that you practiced the A section. Follow the same sound goals outlined in No. 1 above.

4. Learn the A' section the same way that you practiced the A section. Follow the same sound goals outlined above. Be sure that the extra E's at the ends of the phrases are played gently and are tapered.

5. Combine the sections of this piece. You may want to make up your own words to go with the melody to help portray a sad story. Listen carefully to the two-note slurs to be sure that you lean on the first note and taper the end.

Finishing for performance

Ask yourself:

Do you hear the mood of this piece pictured by the title?

Do you hear goals of phrases?

Do you hear two-note slurs played with stress on the first note and taperings at the ends?

Do you hear a smooth and connected melody?

Do you hear both hands shape phrases?

Practice with your ear as your guide in achieving an answer of "yes" to all of these questions.

To the Teacher

Affect/program: student should associate a sad story, real or fictional, to help achieve the mood of "A Sad Story"

Form: A B A'

Balance: single-note melody above single-note accompaniment

Fingering: relatively stationary positions; some extensions to an octave

Coordination: playing of consecutive two-note slurs

This piece helps a student develop:

• playing of two-note slurs

• sustaining skills in playing a long melody

• performance of a slow piece with expression

Notes:

The student should hear the melody in the last section as being the same as that in the first section, with the addition of one note at the end of the original two-note slurs.

Students who do not easily grasp the feeling of this slow expressive style can add words to the melody to tell a tale of a sad story.

March, Op. 39, No. 10   **Kabelevsky**

See *Masterwork Classics 3*, page 42.

To the Teacher

Affect/program: an energetic march in a parade

Form: four four-measure phrases

Balance/voicing: primary consideration is voicing tops of chords

Fingering: quick shifts due to the rhythm

Coordination: rapid playing of chords

This piece helps a student develop:
- quick fingering shifts
- playing of two-note chords
- exactness in playing rhythms

Notes:

Some present-day performers do not lift at the end of two-note slurs here so that the tempo can be quite quick and lively. If the teacher prefers this interpretation, he/she should explain this to the student. Earlier pieces have prepared the student to lift the hand quickly after two-note slurs.

Getting ready to play

This piece can be thought of as an energetic march for young people in a parade. It is marked "energico," "energetically." Do you expect the rhythm to be strong and steady in a march? _____

How long do you expect the phrases to be? _____ It appears that the chords at the end of each line conclude the phrase. Sight-read the melody in the right hand and place brackets around the phrases. Then place an arrow at the focal point of the phrase. Your ear will help tell you where the focal point will be. Usually it comes near the end of a phrase. Sometimes it will be the highest note in the phrase.

How are measures 1-2 different from measures 5-6 ? _____
How are measures 1-2 different from measures 13-14 ? _____

Practicing for performance

Practice step by step. Be sure that you do not move ahead until you have met all of the thought and sound goals for the previous step that you worked on. These goals come from what you have learned about earlier pieces as well as what you find written in the step. Your ear will tell you when you have learned a step well enough to move ahead! At the beginning of your practice the following day, you will want to go back several steps to practice and review what you have learned in earlier practice.

1. Practice this piece by learning all of the like ideas at the same time. This piece has two different ideas in it. Idea <u>a</u> is the rhythmic melody with the dotted quarter notes and the sixteenths. Idea <u>b</u> is the two chords at the ends of the phrases (these chords are called the cadences). Learn idea <u>b</u> first. Isolate the chords at the end of each phrase and practice them, first hands separately, and then hands together. Play them loudly and with strong rhythm. Practice them until you can play them in the performance tempo of the piece.

2. Practice the <u>a</u> motives in this piece. Tap the rhythm for the right hand in measures 1-2. It is important to count sixteenths each time as you practice this piece since the rhythm is intricate. Learn the right hand in measures 1-2. When this is learned well, continue by learning the right hand for measures 5-6, then measures 9-10, then measures 13-14. Now practice the left hand alone in measures 10 and 14. Practice both hands in measures 10 and 14.

3. Practice the first phrase in this piece combining the <u>a</u> and <u>b</u> motives here. Concentrate on and listen for
- exact rhythm
- goals of the phrase
- correct fingering
- strong chords

4. Learn the second, third, and fourth phrases as you did in No. 3 above. Concentrate on the same sound goals.

5. As you strive to combine the phrases, learn the first and second phrases as a group. Then learn the third and fourth phrases as a group. When you have mastered both of these groupings, continue by learning the entire piece as a whole. Listen to be sure that the rhythm is strong and firm.

Finishing for performance

Ask yourself:

Do you hear a steady tempo in your performance?

Do you hear firm cadences—chords—at the ends of the phrases?

Do you hear exact rhythms for the sixteenths and dotted quarter notes?

Do you hear a strong pulse with one beat per measure?

Practice now with the goal of answering "yes" to all of these questions. Your ear will be your guide.

Getting ready to play

The "program" for this piece has been left for the performer's imagination to determine. Notice that the composer has indicated that "A Tale" should be played "moderately." Sight-read the right hand melody and decide on a story that you want this piece to be about. Write several words to describe the story here. _____

Look at this piece to discover how the composer put the phrases together. First search for repetitions of the beginning of the main melody. List the measures where the main melody begins to repeat. _____ This shows the sections of this piece.

- Phrase one   measures 1-4
- Phrase two   measures 5-8 + measures 9-12

Phrase two begins the same as Phrase one but it is extended so that it becomes an eight-measure phrase. The long note in measure 12 with a fermata signals the phrase end.

- Phrase three measures 13-16

This phrase is the same as Phrase one.

Divide this piece into small sections and place arrows at peaks of phrases. Follow the slurs in the music. For each group of notes under a slur, place an arrow at the focal point of that small phrase. This will be the note that the music pulls to in your performance.

Practicing for performance

Practice step by step. Be sure that you do not move ahead until you have met all of the thought and sound goals for the previous step that you worked on. These goals come from what you have learned about earlier pieces as well as what you find written in the step. Your ear will tell you when you have learned a step well enough to move ahead! At the beginning of your practice the following day, you will want to go back several steps to practice and review what you have learned in earlier practice.

1. Practice measures 1-4 first hands separately and then hands together. Concentrate on correct fingering and listen for the goals of the short phrases. The phrases should be rounded in measures 1-2. The phrase in measures 3-4 pulls to the last note. Be sure that you use the correct fingers in the right hand in measure 3.

2. Practice the last five measures in the second phrase, measures 8-12. Notice that your hand position does not change here. When these four measures are learned, add measures 5-7 to this. Correct fingering is especially important. Listen to hear goals of all of the short phrases.

3. Combine the sections of this piece. Listen carefully to be sure that you sneak into the sound at the beginnings of phrases. Also, the ends of many of the phrases should taper. Be certain that the listener can hear the phrase taperings.

Finishing for performance

Ask yourself:

Do you hear a very musical piece with rounded and shaped phrases?

Do you hear the long phrase in the middle of the piece pull and move to its goal?

Do you hear a smooth connected legato?

Do you hear smooth "rallentandos?"

Do you hear one pulse per measure?

Practice with the goal of answering "yes" to all of the questions letting your ear be your guide.

See *Masterwork Classics 3*, page 43.

To the Teacher

Affect/program: student devises a "tale" to go with the music

Form: reappearance of the main theme defines the three sections

Balance/voicing: right hand melody over left hand accompaniment

Fingering: changing of fingers on repeated notes is important in setting hand position for the following part.

Coordination: smooth shifting of fingering

This piece helps a student develop:

- changing fingers on a single note
- attention to rounded phrases
- smooth shifting of fingering and hand position within and between phrases

Notes:

The student should learn to correctly change fingers on a single note in measure 3 in the beginning of practice.

A Tiresome Tale, Op. 98, No. 8   Gretchaninoff

See *Masterwork Classics 3*, page 44.

Getting ready to play

Imagine the way you feel when you are tired and bored. That will be the feeling that you try to give listeners who hear this piece—the feeling of hearing a tale of which they are tired! If something—a word, or in music, a short phrase—is repeated over and over, it becomes tiresome or boring. Look at measures 11-12. You see the motive repeated three times. The composer has indicated that the pianist should play this section "with boredom."

Discover the way this piece is put together—the form. Look for repetitions of the opening measures. Measures 5-8 are like measures 1-4 except for slight changes in measures 7-8. What are the measure numbers where measures 5-8 repeat? _____ What are the measure numbers of the phrase that is entirely different? _____ List the measures below of the form of this piece.

    a   _____
    a'   _____
    b   _____
    a'   _____

Circle the two-note slurs in this piece. The last note of these two-note slurs should not be played staccato. The slurs over the four-note groups in the right hand establish units which should not be separated.

Place brackets around all phrases in the piece. How long might one expect the phrases to be? _____ Phrases in this piece could be two measures or four measures long. Either answer could be correct. Place an arrow above the note in each phrase to which all of the other ones pull.

Practicing for performance

Practice step by step. Be sure that you do not move ahead until you have met all of the thought and sound goals for the previous step that you worked on. These goals come from what you have learned about earlier pieces as well as what you find written in the step. Your ear will tell you when you have learned a step well enough to move ahead! At the beginning of your practice the following day, you will want to go back several steps to practice and review what you have learned in earlier practice.

1. Look for patterns as you begin to practice the a phrase, measures 1-4. In the left hand notice the notes that remain the same and the pattern of the notes that change. Circle the notes that change in measures 1-2 and in measures 3-4. Your eyes should focus on the changing notes rather than the G's and D's. Practice the left hand alone several times. Listen for the two-note slurs. Look for patterns in the right hand of measures 1-4. Practice the right hand alone several times. Listen for goals of phrases and a smooth legato.

2. Combine both hands in measures 1-4, practicing slowly at first and gradually increasing the tempo. Listen for goals of phrases and two-note slurs.

3. Practice a', measures 5-8, following the same procedures as in Nos. 1 and 2 above.

4. Practice the b section, measures 9-12, following the same procedures as in Nos. 1 and 2. Think about how you will play measures 11-12 to make them sound boring. Be careful that the sound achieved here is not too heavy or too loud.

5. Combine the sections of this piece by practicing a and a' and b and a'. Once you can play the piece in two sections achieving the sound goals, work to combine the sections of the entire piece. Listen to be sure that the performance portrays the mood of a "tiresome tale."

Finishing for performance

Ask yourself:

Do you hear the goal of each phrase in the performance?

Do you hear the right hand melody project over the left hand accompaniment?

Do you hear one pulse in each measure?

Do you hear the story suggested by the title given for this piece?

Let the goal of your practice now be to answer "yes" to each of these questions.

To the Teacher

Affect/program: the experience of hearing a tiring tale told through this selection

Form: a a' b a'

Balance/voicing: right hand single-note melody over left hand single-note accompaniment

Fingering: hand positions remain relatively stationary

Coordination: two-note slurs in left hand under continuous and legato right hand melody

This piece helps a student develop:

• progression of events of a story through a piece

• coordination of a moving right hand melody over slower two-note slurs in left hand

Notes:

Accents in the score are for emphasis and should not be played too strongly.

A slight ritard in measures 11-12 can help give the feeling of boredom with the intentional repetitions of the motive.

A Lingering Song, Op. 98, No.14   **Gretchaninoff**

See *Masterwork Classics 3*, page 45.

Getting ready to play

This piece could be about a song that lingers in your mind or memory. It might have the kind of tune that you would hum gently or silently all day long! You can expect to find that kind of tune in this piece. Sight-read the right hand melody and write a word to help describe this feeling and the mood you want this piece to have.

_____

Place open brackets around the phrases. Then place an arrow above the magnet note in each phrase.

The same theme occurs three times. List the measures here that repeat the theme. _____ _____ _____ Only the last measure is different each time. Write the total number of new measures that you will need to learn for this piece in this blank.

_____

To help learn this last measure and to help memorize it, write the first right hand note in this last measure of the phrase.

first right hand note

line one	last measure	_____
line two	last measure	_____
line three	last measure	_____

Circle the two-note slurs in your music. When you practice, remember to lean on the first note and gently taper the second.

Measures 9-13 are the only contrasting music in the entire piece. Do you think measure 13 might be a reflection of measure 12? Or a sigh? _____ Think about how you will interpret this part when you play it.

Practicing for performance

Practice step by step. Be sure that you do not move ahead until you have met all of the thought and sound goals for the previous step that you worked on. These goals come from what you have learned about earlier pieces as well as what you find written in the step. Your ear will tell you when you have learned a step well enough to move ahead! At the beginning of your practice the following day, you will want to go back several steps to practice and review what you have learned in earlier practice.

1. Practice the right hand alone in measures 1-4. Notice the length of the slurs that the composer has written in. The first slur is quite long, followed by the last ones which are short. As you learn the right hand alone, be certain that your playing shows the listener where the slurs are written in the music. Observe the dynamic markings. After playing the left hand several times alone, combine both hands for this phrase. Continue to listen to hear the phrase markings written in the music and to hear the goals of the phrases.

2. Learn measures 5-8 by practicing measure 8 alone first. Then practice measures 7-8 as a group. Finally practice all of this line, still listening to be sure that the sound goals from No. 1 are being met.

3. Learn the last repetition of the main theme, measures 14-17. Practice in the same way that you did in No. 2 above.

4. To learn the section that is different, measures 9-13, first practice each hand alone. Listen to hear the two-note slurs taper and to play to the goal of the phrases. Then practice in groups of two measures, measures 9-10 and measures 11-12. Finally, connect both of these groups and add measure 13, the measure that has the "sigh."

5. Combine these smaller groups of phrases into larger sections. Practice measures 1-8 as a section and measures 9-17 as a section. Continue to listen for the playing to pull to goals of phrases and for the two-note slurs to taper.

6. Practice the entire piece. Aim to hear in your performance
- long left hand staccato quarters
- balance of melody and accompaniment
- tapered ends of two-note slurs
- goals of phrases

Finishing for performance

Ask yourself:

Do you hear goals of phrases?

Do you hear two pulses for each measure rather than four?

Do you hear the dynamic plan written in the music come alive in your performance?

Do you hear a smooth legato for the notes placed under the long slurs?

Do you hear left hand staccatos that are not short, but are about the length of eighth notes (one-half of their written value)?

Do you hear the right hand melody sing out over the left hand accompaniment?

Practice now with your ear as your guide until you can answer "yes" to each of these questions.

To the Teacher

Affect/program: a melancholy singer

Balance/voicing: right hand melody above single- and double-note accompaniment

Fingering: relatively stationary hand positions

Coordination: interpretation of slurs of varying lengths in a long line

This piece helps a student develop:
- the sustaining of a long melody line
- balance of melody and thick accompaniment

Notes:

Students should be able to verbally articulate the differences between measures 5, 8, and 17 as an aid to memory.

It is important that a smooth legato be achieved with even gradation of crescendos and diminuendos in the melody.

The short slurs should not get in the way of the long line.

The Bear

See *Masterwork Classics 3*, page 46.

See *Masterwork Classics 3*, page 47.

Getting ready to play

The title of this piece is a programmatic one. Knowing that it is about a bear, you already have a preconceived thought about what kinds of sounds it might have. Notice that the left hand plays the same two notes, an F broken octave, throughout the entire piece in a very low, growling register of the piano. A figure that is repeated persistently is called an "ostinato."

Sight-read the top note of the right hand line to hear the melody. Place open brackets around the phrases in this piece. Measures 1-2 seem to be an introduction. Did you find any phrases that were not four measures long?_____ Place an arrow above the magnet note in each phrase.

Measures 3-6 and measures 7-10 are almost exactly alike. Circle the note in the second phrase that is different from the first phrase.

Compare the next two phrases. Are they exactly alike? _____ Compare the last two phrases, measures 19-26 with measures 3-10. Are they exactly alike? _____ How many different measures will you have to learn to play this piece? _____

Write the dynamic signs and any other markings for the introduction and each phrase.

introduction	_____
phrase one	_____
phrase two	_____
phrase three	_____
phrase four	_____
phrase five	_____
phrase six	_____

Remember to play the tenuto markings (—) with a stress.

Practicing for performance

Practice step by step. Be sure that you do not move ahead until you have met all of the thought and sound goals for the previous step that you worked on. These goals come from what you have learned about earlier pieces as well as what you find written in the step. Your ear will tell you when you have learned a step well enough to move ahead! At the beginning of your practice the following day, you will want to go back several steps to practice and review what you have learned in earlier practice.

1. Practice the left hand ostinato to gain a feeling for playing broken octaves. Place a slight stress on the lowest note of each octave. Play the thumb very lightly. Practice the crescendo in measures 1-2.

2. Practice the right hand alone in the first phrase. Then combine both hands. Practice to achieve light left hand staccatos and to hear the goal of the phrase. Continue by practicing the second phrase since it is almost exactly the same as the first phrase.

3. Follow the same procedure for practicing the third phrase as you did in No. 2. The fourth phrase is exactly the same except that the dynamic level is different. Practice both of these phrases as a section, hearing the difference in dynamics as well as the accomplishment of the sound goals mentioned above.

4. Since the last section is the same as the first section, begin now to practice this piece as a whole. Listen carefully for
- light left hand accompaniment
- melody in right hand to project over left hand accompaniment
- the dynamic plan of the entire piece
- goals of the phrases

Finishing for performance

Ask yourself:

Do you hear melody project over the accompaniment?

Do you hear the first note of each pair in the left hand slightly accented?

Do you hear goals of phrases?

Do you hear the dynamic differences written in the music?

Practice now with your ear guiding you until you can answer "yes" to each of these questions.

To the Teacher

Affect/program: a bear lumbering nearby and in the distance

Form: motive repeated six times with slight variations

Balance/voicing: right hand melody over low left hand broken octaves

Fingering: relatively stationary positions; left hand broken octaves

Coordination: develops independence of rhythmic figures between the hands

This piece helps a student develop:
- voicing of melody above accompaniment in low register
- coordination of independent rhythmic figures between the hands
- playing broken octaves

March, Op. 98, No. 3   Gretchaninoff

See *Masterwork Classics 3*, page 48.

Getting ready to play

What tempo and feeling (affect) would be expected from a march? _____ The indication "marziale" means "martial" or "pompous and disciplined." This piece might be for soldiers who are marching. Would you expect the rhythm for this piece to be strong and stately? _____

Place brackets around the phrases. Although these phrases to be two measures long, they could also be interpreted as four-measure phrases. Place an arrow at the focal point of each phrase.

Discover the form. Look for repetitions of phrases. Write the measures in each section below.

a	_____
a'	_____
b	_____
b	_____
a'	_____

What is the difference between a and a'? _____ How many different measures will you need to learn in this piece? _____

Circle the two-note slurs.

Practicing for performance

Practice step by step. Be sure that you do not move ahead until you have met all of the thought and sound goals for the previous step that you worked on. These goals come from what you have learned about earlier pieces as well as what you find written in the step. Your ear will tell you when you have learned a step well enough to move ahead! At the beginning of your practice the following day, you will want to go back several steps to practice and review what you have learned in earlier practice.

1. Practice the a phrase, measures 1-4, first. Play only the first three beats in measure 1 hands together. Learn this motive well. You will notice that this motive is the same in the next measure. Once you have learned this short motive, add the last eighth note in measure 1 and combine both hands in measures 1-2. Continue by learning measures 3-4. Be especially careful to play the left hand fingering in measure 4 exactly right! Combine both parts of the a section thinking about and listening carefully for the following:
   - goals of phrases
   - two-note slurs
   - correct fingering

2. Learn phrase a'. Practice measures 7-8 first since these are the only measures that are different from a. Then practice all of a' as a phrase.

3. Continue by practicing a and a' as a section. Work for the same sound and thought goals as outlined in No. 1.

4. Practice measures 9-10. Work on them briefly hands separately if necessary. Listen carefully for the "non legato" and check for the fingering in measure 10. Continue by practicing measures 11-12. Listen and check for the same goals here.

5. Notice the dynamic difference between <u>b</u> measures 9-12 and <u>b</u> measures 13-16. Practice both <u>b</u> sections listening this dynamic change. Then practice these sections combined with the last <u>a</u>' section. Work on this part of the piece listening for
- goals of phrases
- dynamic differences
- two-note slurs that taper
- non-legato that is not too short

6. Cadences are chords that end a phrase and firmly set the key center. Strong cadences in this piece occur in measures 4, 8, 12, 16. Practice all four of these measures in a row. Listen to hear how the chords firmly establish the end of the phrase.

7. Combine all sections of this piece. Listen carefully for the accomplishment of the sound goals in No. 5 above and for strong cadences. Be certain that the rhythm is strong but not filled with accents. Listen to hear that your performance is "martial."

Finishing for performance

Ask yourself:

Does your performance sound like a march?

Do you hear goals of phrases?

Do you hear two-note slurs taper gently?

Do you hear dynamic contrast between sections?

Do you hear "non-legato" where it is written in the music?

Do you hear each phrase begin with the sound easing in and moving toward the focal note of the phrase?

Practice now with your ear guiding your practice so that you can answer "yes" to all of these questions.

To the Teacher

Affect/program: soldiers marching in a parade

Form: <u>a</u> <u>a'</u> <u>b</u> <u>b</u> <u>a'</u>

Balance/voicing: right hand melody, often in double notes, voiced above left hand accompaniment

Fingering: hands remain relatively stationary; crossings in measures 12 and 16 need attention

Coordination: voicing of melody above thick texture in note-against-note style

This piece helps a student develop:
- rounding of short phrases
- voicing thick texture

Notes:

Students should begin phrases without accents on the first note of that phrase. This practice guide often refers to the concept of "sneaking" or "easing" into the sound at the beginning of a phrase. This "sneaking" would apply to all phrases in this piece.

Non-legato tones in measures 9-10 and corresponding places should be light and played like eighth notes rather than as very short sounds.

Alfred's Basic Piano Library

Willard A. Palmer • Morton Manus • Amanda Vick Lethco

A PIANO COURSE
FOR BEGINNERS OF ALL AGES

Alfred's Basic Piano Library offers nine perfectly graded beginning series which are designed to prepare students of all ages for a successful musical learning experience. With the exception of **Alfred's Basic Adult Piano Course,** which is complete in itself, all of the beginning series are interchangeable at several levels (see arrows below), and lead into the main **Alfred's Basic** course, which is complete through Level 6 (seven levels all together). This course, then, is the most flexible of any method in allowing the teacher to personally design a specific curriculum according to the age and needs of each individual student. On completion, the student is ready to begin playing the great piano masterworks.

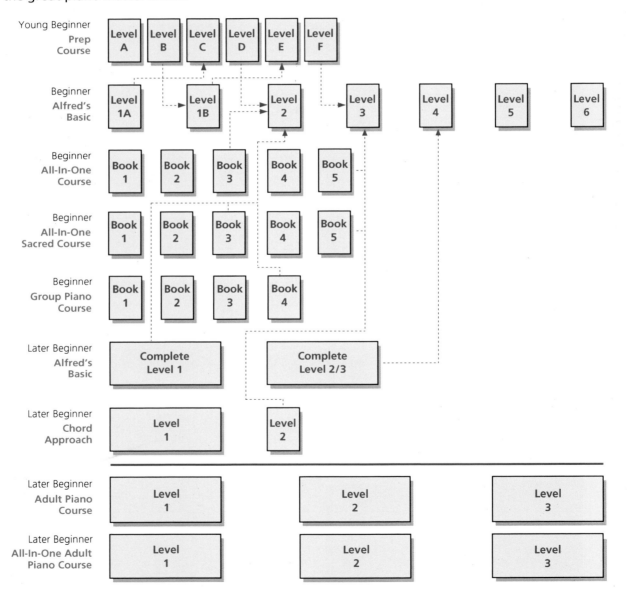

alfred.com

167

$11.95 in USA

ISBN-10: 0-7390-1379-3
ISBN-13: 978-0-7390-1379-3

9 780739 013793

0 38081 02023 5

ISBN 0-7390-1379-3

FOUR STAR
SIGHT READING AND EAR TESTS

DAILY EXERCISES FOR PIANO STUDENTS

BY BORIS BERLIN and ANDREW MARKOW

Series Editor
SCOTT McBRIDE SMITH

FREDERICK
HARRIS
MUSIC

The Frederick Harris Music Co., Limited
(905) 501-1595
Fax (905) 501-0929
Printed in Canada

Unit 1, 5865 McLaughlin Road
Mississauga, Ontario
Canada   L5R 1B8
Imprimé au Canada

www.frederickharrismusic.com

We acknowledge the financial support of the Government of Canada through the Book Publishing Industry Development Program (BPIDP) for our publishing activities.